"As a college student, I was challer̲_____ Panosian in a required class called t̲l_____.…__, u.ı vvestern Civilization. I will never forget the passion of Dr. Panosian's teaching of history and the clarity with which he taught about two different world views that have defined our past. He instilled into me a love for history and how it can inform us as we address the challenges of this generation. Chris Anderson has written a compelling story that is much more than the biography of a humble but significant person in the field of education. His book tells the story of an oppressed people and the new opportunities in America that not only changed the life of Dr. Panosian but also influenced thousands because of his teaching. Ed Panosian began each class with 'a moment of review and then on we go.' After you read this book, you will be more informed about the past and more inspired for the future."

— **Asa Hutchinson**, Governor of Arkansas

"What a story! What a man! What a life! I can see Dr. Panosian in my mind riding his bicycle, smiling with grace toward all his students, and standing before his class as if he were an actor on stage. I'll never forget his lectures in my two semesters of Church History. Ed Panosian represents the best of Bob Jones University in every way. A compelling life message of a true giant!"

— **Steve Pettit**, president of Bob Jones University, Greenville, South Carolina

"Part of true piety is not only honoring God, but also giving honor to whom honor is due. A servant of Christ like Edward Panosian rarely receives honor in this life. Here, Chris Anderson writes as a friend and former student, granting readers an interesting glimpse into this honorable man's life, times, family, and work. Anderson honors Panosian, but he does not glorify him. That distinction is reserved for the Master Whom Panosian and Anderson both serve. If God is glorified by the faithful service of His saints, then He is the Hero of Panosian's story."

— **Kevin Bauder**, professor at Central Baptist Theological Seminary, Minneapolis

"Among all the gifts given by the Holy Spirit to believers, there is none more useful and variegated than the gift of teaching. Dr. Panosian is a brilliant teacher with an extraordinary ability to make historical figures come alive. Now, we have the remarkable story of his life and the amazing Providence that prepared him for such a unique ministry, skillfully brought to life in writing by another gifted teacher, Pastor Chris Anderson."

— **Phil Johnson**, executive director of Grace to You

Chris Anderson with Ed Panosian, 2018; photo by Zuly Rabelo

PANOSIAN

A Story of God's Gracious Providence

CHRIS ANDERSON

Copy Editor: Abby Huffstutler
Layout Designer: Jared Miller
Art Director: Joe Tyrpak

Cover Design: Joe Tyrpak; front cover photo by Stephen Dysert, 2017, courtesy of Bob Jones University; back cover photo of Dr. Panosian, 1981, courtesy of Bob Jones University; back cover photo of Chris Anderson, 2013, courtesy of Jared Miller.

First printing 2018

ISBN 978-0-9961605-9-9

for Ed and Betty Panosian

CONTENTS

GOD'S GRACIOUS PROVIDENCE

*"What are thought to be chance occurrences are
just so many proofs of heavenly providence,
especially of fatherly kindness."*

—John Calvin[1]

"I being in the way, the LORD led me."[2]

Those who have sat under the teaching ministry of Dr. Panosian for even a short time have doubtless heard him borrow the ancient testimony of Abraham's servant as his own. Genesis 24:27 rejoices in God's providence—His orchestration of even minor events to accomplish His purposes. With apologies to the Bard, there are no "slings and arrows of outrageous fortune."[3] God is sovereign over everything, from international affairs to personal affections. Even when we are unaware of it (as most of the world is), God is ordering even the minute details of the universe to accomplish His purpose and display His glory.

Dr. Panosian has taught thousands that the fingerprints of the sovereign God are all over human history. More than twenty years ago he wrote the following regarding the benefits of history for the Christian student:

> If history is the record of God's incessant supervision over men and nations—the memorial of God's mercies, His blessings for obedi-

[1] John Calvin, *Institutes of the Christian Religion,* ed. John T. McNeill. trans. Ford Lewis Battles (Philadelphia: Westminster Press, 1960) I: 60.

[2] Genesis 24:27 KJV.

[3] Barbara Mowat, Paul Werstine, Michael Poston, Rebecca Niles, eds., *Hamlet* (Washington: Folger Shakespeare Library, n.d.), accessed August 27, 2018. www.folgerdigitaltexts.org.

ence and His judgment for disobedience, the working out of His sovereign pleasure ruling and overruling the free but responsible wills of men—then it is to be studied because of what it *is*.

History shows the providence of God—His "seeing before"—on behalf of His people.[4]

Ed Panosian's story is a story of God's providence.

Most know Dr. Edward M. Panosian as a professor at Bob Jones University in Greenville, South Carolina, where he taught history for over half a century. Dr. Panosian is an icon. His wisdom, his passion, his appearance, his wit, his impossibly patient speaking pace, and his voice—what a *voice!*—all combine to make him a larger-than-life legend. He has taught more students than any other professor in the history of BJU. He is almost universally respected. But he is not well known—as a *man*, I mean, not an icon. My goal is to remedy that.

———

The Panosian story is challenging to tell. It is the story of a man, but it is also the story of his ancestors, their homeland, and their oppressors. In fact, the book will be roughly half over before its principal character is even born! The two halves of the story may feel like two very different books that have been pasted together. They are not. Dr. Panosian and I believe that understanding his story is impossible without understanding the story of his parents and their nearly miraculous survival. For that reason, inserted throughout the story are pertinent histories of the Armenians, of the declining Ottoman Empire[5], of World War I, and of the Armenian Genocide (1915–1920). These

———

[4] Edward Panosian, "A Case for History in the Christian School" in *The Providence of God in History* (Greenville, SC: BJU Press, 1996), 2–3.

[5] By the year 1900, the once vast Ottoman Empire had been dismembered and distributed among the greater nations of Europe. What remained was essentially modern-day Turkey. Throughout the book, the terms "Ottoman Empire" and "Turkey" are used interchangeably. At points in the book, the Panosians or newspapers refer to their homeland as "Syria" or "Syrian Turkey" or even "Armenia." The borders in that region of the world have shifted significantly in the last century. While the other designations aren't inaccurate, this book will typically refer to the homeland of Dr. Panosian's parents as "Turkey" or "the Ottoman Empire."

aren't diversions from the history of the Panosian family; they are intrinsic to it.[6]

Much of the Panosian story takes place in Turkey. I was greatly helped by a trip I took to Turkey in 2008, little knowing that that journey was preparing me for this one. More providence! Even more helpful, in the months surrounding the writing of this book I consumed many insightful resources on the Armenian Genocide and World War I, which I often cite in footnotes. I have relied upon many respected historians, but I found four books to be especially helpful:

- *Armenia's Golgotha,* the memoirs of genocide survivor Grigoris Balakian which provide an eyewitness account of the Turks' treachery.
- *The Burning Tigris,* written by Grigoris Balakian's great-nephew, Peter Balakian. This is perhaps the most thorough book on the history of the genocide, beautifully written by an author who won a Pulitzer Prize in 2016 for his poetry.
- *Ambassador Morgenthau's Story,* a firsthand account of the genocide, written by the U.S. Ambassador to Turkey during the genocide. This is especially useful because it was written by a respected American official and because Morgenthau is neither an Armenian, nor a Christian, and therefore cannot be charged with either of those biases as an author. Morgenthau labored valiantly (though ultimately in vain) to protect the Armenians.
- *The Forty Days of Musa Dagh,* an epic (900-page) historical novel by noted Austrian author Franz Werfel, published in 1933. The book did a great deal to make the public aware of the terrors of the genocide during the years following World War I.

---

[6] Dates at the beginning of each chapter in this book are significant. Because the book follows multiple characters in multiple locations and times, the chapters are not strictly chronological.

Ironically, Morgenthau and Werfel were both Jews, and their writings about the genocide are haunting in light of the horrors which their own people would face less than a generation later.

The details of the genocide are grotesque, and they are hard to read. Grigoris Balakian believed that the terrors the Armenians suffered at the hands of the Turks were unprecedented—"the likes of which had never before been recorded in even the bloodiest pages of history."[7] The cruelty of which humans are capable is apt evidence of our depravity. I've shared enough details to accurately depict the terrors of the genocide without piling story upon story in sickening succession. If the details I share seem excessive, know that I exercised considerable restraint.

Although the book describes unthinkable cruelty, it would be unjust to paint all Turks or all Muslims with one broad brush. When I speak of the atrocities of "the Turks," I do so with an eye on the leaders of the Ottoman Empire at the turn of the twentieth century when the genocide took place. It would be unfair to characterize an entire nation by the actions of its leaders, much less by the actions of leaders who ruled one hundred years ago. To repurpose Romans 9:6, "not all Turks are 'Turks'" as I use that term in this book. Humane Turks and kind Muslims existed then as now, as the book will demonstrate.

Along those lines, one might wonder what Dr. Panosian feels toward those responsible for the deaths of many of his family members and the decimation of his people. He provided the answer in a booklet he authored fifteen years before I undertook this project:

> I hate no one except the Devil and his works, though in the flesh I might have reason to hate.... While I am an Armenian-American, I have no hatred. I am a redeemed Christian. My parents came to know the Lord. I hate no one.[8]

Whenever possible, I have quoted Dr. Panosian directly. The man is a master communicator, and it is my hope that those who read his

---

[7] Grigoris Balakian, *Armenia's Golgotha*, trans. Peter Balakian (New York: Vintage, 2009), 48.
[8] Edward M. Panosian, *Islam and the Bible: Considering Islam Biblically* (Greenville, SC: Emerald House, 2003), 1–2.

words—especially those who know his voice—will imagine actually hearing him again.

As I interviewed the Panosians and asked their close acquaintances to share their memories, I realized that there are scores of former students who have vivid memories of things Dr. Panosian said and did. I used social media to reach out to graduates of BJU, asking them to share some of their favorite recollections of Dr. Panosian. I was unprepared for the deluge of nostalgia, affection, and gratitude that my request unleashed. For thousands of people, the Panosian story feels very much like their own story—that's the depth of attachment they feel. For that reason, I have sprinkled many of their memories throughout the book. Their fondness for their beloved professor reminded me what a privilege and responsibility was mine to be researching and writing this book. I hope it will inform and inspire readers, whether or not they are already familiar with Ed Panosian.

The Panosian story needed to be told while its principal character was still able to share it. It is one of suffering and survival, of cruelty and courage. Above all, it is a story of God's gracious providence. As Dr. Panosian has reminded us again and again, "History is *His story*." May He be glorified through its telling! *Soli Deo Gloria!*

PART ONE

"IN GREEN PASTURES"

CHAPTER ONE

A PIN CUSHION TO PRIZE

1987 — ELMIRA, NEW YORK

"Behold also the ships, which though they be so great, and are driven of fierce winds, yet are they turned about with a very small helm, whithersoever the governor listeth."

—James 3:4

Little objects may contain massive memories. That's true in this story.

An egg. A pouch of tobacco. A dried fig. A coal box. A shoe. A collection of jewelry. A sum of not quite $25. An assassin's bullet. A fistful of candy. A stick. A magazine advertisement. A perfectly fitted costume. A doctor's prescription. A hospital bed. A bicycle or two. A custom-made chair. A scrapbook. Some 3x5 index cards. And most important of all, a pin cushion.

Sara Panosian, the mother of Ed Panosian, entered paradise on March 2, 1987, almost three months after her family had gathered around her to celebrate her eighty-fifth birthday. She underwent surgery to treat her stomach cancer, and she awoke in the presence of her Savior. On a shelf in her home sat her most prized worldly possession: a simple pin cushion. Her son describes it, slowly, his voice swelling and cracking with emotion:

> It was a little pin cushion—a sewing cushion—which looked like an apple, made of felt, stiffened. It had a removable top, and inside were pins and so forth. She kept it to her dying day.

Sara Panosian—Sara Momjian before her marriage to Nazar Panosian—had seen brutal and beautiful things during her eighty-five years on earth. She had witnessed the worst and best that human beings could do. She had experienced unspeakable sorrows and unexpected joys.

So what made this object, a simple pin cushion, such a treasure?

It held more than pins. It held *hope,* and it had for almost eighty years.

CHAPTER TWO

TWO UNFORGETTABLE HOURS

2017 — ATLANTA, GEORGIA
AND GREENVILLE, SOUTH CAROLINA

"I like this idea. I think it's something I can do. Now . . . tell me how."

—Ed Panosian

My friendship with Dr. Panosian is a recent one. Yes, I was introduced to him in 1990, when I enrolled at Bob Jones University and had him as my professor for a History of Civilization course, along with hundreds of other freshmen.[9] For the next seven years, I saw him around campus, watched him in Shakespearean plays, and heard him perform narrations that would make James Earl Jones jealous. But I didn't know him. He certainly didn't know me. Along with thousands of other students, I felt a deep affection for Dr. Panosian. But I didn't know "Ed."

By the time we became friends, two of my daughters were students at BJU. Astonishingly to me, they didn't have any awareness of the man who in my mind was part of the very fabric of the institution. When Rebekah and Rachel arrived as students in 2015 and 2017, he had already enjoyed over a decade of his well-deserved retirement. They had no real reason to know him. That chapter of the university's story had closed—or almost closed. In God's good providence, an event in 2017 allowed me to reconnect with Dr. Panosian. As a result, we're adding a bit more to that not-quite-closed chapter, for the benefit of both my generation and my daughters'.

---

[9] History of Civilization is known at BJU, where Dr. Panosian taught for over fifty years, as "History of Civ," the title that will be used throughout the rest of this book.

The year 2017 marked the five-hundredth anniversary of the Protestant Reformation, and Killian Hill Baptist Church in Atlanta, Georgia, where I pastor, planned to celebrate the occasion with a Bible conference. I wanted a two-pronged approach: a historian would teach on the events of the Reformation, and a theologian would preach on the *doctrines* of the Reformation, summarized as the "Five Solas"—*Sola Scriptura, Sola Fide, Sola Gratia, Solus Christus,* and *Soli Deo Gloria.* I secured a respected theologian to preach. Now I needed a church historian. Who better to ask than Dr. Panosian? To be honest, I checked with some mutual friends to be sure that he was still physically and mentally up to the task. He was eighty-seven, after all. Assured by them that he was as lucid as ever, I extended the invitation, and he readily accepted. During the conference we were treated to exceptional preaching from Phil Johnson of Grace to You Ministries and riveting history from Ed Panosian.[10] Their speaking styles complemented each other so well. Dr. Panosian is patient, measured, and dramatic. Phil Johnson is an absolute machine gun of exegetical insights. We learned a great deal, and Christ was exalted.

Several former students who attended the conference were struck with the fact that Dr. Panosian was essentially unchanged from the time of their instruction, whether twenty years ago or sixty. He was still both refined and kind—still both august and humble—still the consummate gentleman.

Following the conference, I volunteered to drive Dr. Panosian from Atlanta back to his home in Greenville, South Carolina. I arrived at the hotel to find Dr. Panosian waiting in the lobby. He was early; I was not. I believe I was wearing jeans; he certainly was not. But he greeted me like we were old friends: "Ah, Chris! So good to see you! Thank you for taking time from your busy schedule to get me back to my home." *Warm and courteous as ever,* I thought. As I helped him with his luggage, he handed me a pile of carefully written cards—thank you notes to everyone who had hosted him during the conference. He

---

[10] A recording of each message can be found at sermonaudio.com/khbc.

asked me to have the stamped envelopes addressed and mailed out by the church secretary. How thoughtful. How exquisitely polite!

Typical, I thought. Or at least typical of Dr. Panosian, if not of most people in our day of texts, emails, and emojis.

It was during the two-hour drive north on I-85 that one of my favorite college professors became one of my friends. An icon became a man. Dr. Panosian became Ed. Well, that's not really true; I still feel uncomfortable calling him Ed. But I got to know *him*.

Shortly after our departure, I asked him to tell me his story: "I would love to hear about your family . . . how you came to Christ . . . what brought you to BJU, and what kept you there." I had no idea what I set in motion with that request. For the next two hours, I was transported to the years surrounding World War I—to Turkey, to an orphanage in Beirut, Lebanon, and eventually to Ellis Island, under the watchful eyes of the Statue of Liberty. He told the history of his family with deep emotion and dramatic flair, for an audience of one.

I learned that Dr. Panosian's story is inseparable from the larger story of his people, the Armenians. His name, like the name of almost all Armenians, displays his heritage. He explained: "The 'ian' means 'son of' and is the patronym of all Armenians. I am *Panos* —the son of Panos—meaning, Stephen." Explaining the meaning behind his name provided him with an irresistible opportunity to display his winsome, self-deprecating humor: "The obvious emphasis of 'Panosian' is on the *nose!*" I smiled, and again I muttered in my mind: *Typical.*

Dr. Panosian is unashamedly Armenian. To be honest, until the last few years, I had no idea who the Armenians were, or are, other than jokes that confused them with the theological opponents of Calvinists—the Arminians. But the story of the Armenian people should be known. It is filled with horrors and heroes, with persecution and perseverance.

During that car ride, I heard harrowing episodes from the Armenian Genocide, the calculating work of Turkish Muslims to eliminate Armenians from the face of the earth. By the end of World War I, one and a half *million* Armenians had been murdered in what is sometimes called "the hidden holocaust."[11] I learned that most of Ed Panosian's forebears were slain in the ethnic cleansing perpetrated by the Ottoman Empire. And I learned that his parents only narrowly—and providentially—escaped with their lives.

My ignorance of these events was an embarrassment to me. I'm reasonably well-read. And yet, for most of my life, I hadn't heard or read anything about the Armenian Genocide. In contrast, I have known about the Jewish Holocaust of World War II since I was a young boy. I learned of it in classes, in museums, and in dramatic presentations like *The Diary of Anne Frank*, Corrie Ten Boom's *The Hiding Place*, and the 1970s television miniseries *Holocaust*, which left a deep impression on me as an elementary student. But Armenians and their suffering surrounding World War I? I was completely uninformed. Mercy, I was uninformed *despite having traveled to Turkey* and despite studying its history and sites beforehand![12]

I would never suggest that the world has been too mindful of the Jewish Holocaust. But we have neglected the tragic plight and heroic fight of the Armenians. Indeed, to this day, the Turkish government denies that the genocide even happened. The Armenian holocaust should be known. Dr. Panosian and I hope this book can help to rectify that, at least in a small way.

Driving Dr. Panosian home that day in 2017 was a divine appointment, another example of God's good providence. My only regret later was that I didn't record the conversation. But I had an idea. Truth be told, I have a hundred ideas a day . . . about two of which are actually feasible. But this was a great one! I told Dr. Panosian that this story must be shared. I asked him to consider allowing me to write his biography, starting with the story of his parents' escape from Turkey. He

---

[11] Peter Balakian, *The Burning Tigris* (New York, Perennial, 2004), xiii.

[12] In my defense, the three guidebooks I have on Turkey are painstaking in their effort to avoid mentioning the Armenian Genocide, presumably in deference to the Republic of Turkey. For example, John Freely's book *Istanbul: The Imperial City,* says nothing of the slaughter of 1.5 million Armenians. The closest Freely comes in the book's almost 400 pages is to record that 6,000 Armenians were killed "in reprisals" for an attack carried out by "Armenian terrorists" on August 26, 1896. John Freely, *Istanbul: The Imperial City* (London: Penguin, 1998), 287.

said he would give it some thought. I dropped him off, thanked him for the riveting conversation, and we both went about our lives.

Just over a month later, I watched a beautiful, disturbingly vivid movie about the Armenian Genocide called *The Promise*. I was captivated. Because it has some objectionable elements, I can recommend it only with reservations. But it fanned the flames of my interest in the story of Ed Panosian's family. What I had heard on the two-hour car ride I now saw in a two-hour movie. The film nudged me again to pursue the Panosian project.

I immediately wrote Dr. Panosian an email—my preferred means of communication during our months of collaboration, not his, though he has been more than accommodating. I expressed my zeal to tell his story. I asked for an interview, and he agreed. Within the week, we were seated together in South Carolina in his home on the back campus of Bob Jones University. He greeted me at the door with his customary warmth and enthusiasm. He took my jacket and led me into the living room—a room that feels exactly like you'd expect a history professor's home to feel, complete with fascinating décor, beautiful rugs, elegant antiques, and black and white photos. Predictably, the Panosian home echoes with the perpetual tick-tick-ticking of a grandfather clock, a soothing and sobering reminder of the relentless passing of time.

We settled onto his couch, and he prepared to tell his story to me again—this time with a recorder between us. I prayed, asking the Lord to bless our endeavor. Then, in his inimitable voice, he started the conversation with two declaratives and an imperative: "I like this idea. I think it's something I can do. Now . . . tell me how."

For the next two hours he took me again to Turkey, telling me of his family, their experiences, and their personalities. This time he was ready with notes he had jotted down, anecdotes our conversation had brought to his recollection, and a century-old picture of his mother. Multiple times during the conversation, his voice betrayed his emotion, especially when speaking of his father. Listening to those talks again while working on the book has been a joy.

He mentioned as an aside that his wife Betty—"the American" as his mother had called her—knew as much of his family's history as he did. His mother had taken Betty into her confidence during times when Ed was off with his brothers or cousins, leaving the ladies home with plenty of time to visit. Betty was entrusted with details that few other family members had heard.

I knew Betty Panosian as my "Storytelling" professor during my undergrad years at BJU. She has a sweet intensity to her. She's a small lady, but she is unmistakably strong. My favorite, somewhat humiliating memory of her class involved a speech I was assigned to give. I was to tell a children's story which took place on a farm. *How hard could it be?* I thought, not realizing that my teacher—my judge—had a lifetime of experience reading stories to children.

I began, reading the farm story much as I would have read Chaucer or Shakespeare or the classified ads. I could immediately tell that she wasn't impressed. I had learned in freshman speech to read my audience's nonverbal cues. Her furrowed brow was a bit unsettling, but I forged ahead, trying to appear undaunted. I came to a portion where an unusually wise hen speaks, and I read the hen's lines in my normal voice. Mrs. Panosian had heard enough. She cut me off, almost offended: "That is not what a hen sounds like. If you want to hold your audience's attention, you need to *become your character!* Make us *believe* you!" Her voice had risen with passion, but just as quickly, it returned to normal. Kindly, she instructed me to try again. It didn't go especially well. She wasn't satisfied until I had set aside my inhibitions and read the lines—ridiculously, I thought—in the voice of a hen. It taught me as much about my own pride as about the craft of storytelling. Diminutive Professor: 1. Mortified Student: 0.

During a brief break in my interview with Dr. Panosian, we enjoyed some refreshments Mrs. Panosian had prepared: cookies and our choice of coffee or tea, all served on nice dishes. *Typical,* I thought again. I asked her if she would be willing to help with this project. She deadpanned that her schedule was "*sooo* busy these days." In her retirement she spends most of her time in her home. She said she would be glad to offer me whatever help she could.

Within three days, I had again driven north to Greenville, and I was back in their home, recorder in hand. I interviewed them together this time, seated at their dining room table. Whenever I listen to the recording, several things make me smile. I was delighted by how they prodded each other's memories. I was surprised at how often we all laughed. And I was thankful for their eagerness to help. Mrs. Panosian had an appointment, and I kept offering to wrap things up so she wouldn't be late. "We still have some time," Dr. Panosian insisted. I tried again a few minutes later. "I'm watching," he said. "We still have ten minutes." And yet once more. "We can continue for five more minutes. It will only take me a few minutes to get her to her appointment." He was enjoying this, and so was I. It was an afternoon I'll not soon forget.

This book is their story, and they've shared it graciously and lucidly, though they are both well into their ninth decade of life. Sitting between them at their dining room table, I knew I was uniquely privileged. I was writing about an amazing portion of world history with a legendary history professor. I was writing a moving story with an accomplished storytelling professor. And all the while, I was unearthing the untold testimony of *the* Edward M. Panosian—a treasure of my alma mater and a giant of the faith.

The only hesitation that either of the Panosians showed during the writing process was a deep desire that Christ, not they, be magnified. Throughout our time together, both were genuinely embarrassed by all the attention. Several months into the project, as we regularly exchanged emails, Dr. Panosian reminded me, "I wish only for heaven's honor." It had been so from our earliest meetings together. That afternoon around their family table, Mrs. Panosian expressed the same desire to be rewarded in heaven, not on earth. And in response, her husband recalled the epitaph that Dr. Bob Jones Jr. had written for his father's funeral: "His record is on high."

Panosian concurred with Dr. Jones: "That's where it matters." Our mutual desire, then, is expressed perfectly by the psalmist: "Not unto us, O LORD, not unto us, but unto Thy name give glory" (Psalm 115:1).

PART TWO

"IN THE PRESENCE OF MINE ENEMIES"

CHAPTER THREE

A PROUD AND PERSEVERING PEOPLE

THE PAST 3,000 YEARS — ARMENIA

"No one remembers the Armenians but the Armenians."

—Dawn Anahid MacKeen[13]

"History had long been unkind to Armenia, which in ancient times was the most powerful independent kingdom on the eastern border of the Roman Empire and in the fourth century became the first nation to make Christianity its official religion."

—G. J. Meyer[14]

Although they didn't know each other, Ed Panosian's parents—Nazar Panosian and Sara Momjian—were both born to families who were part of the Armenian minority in Turkey, the decaying remnant of the once great Ottoman Empire. Armenians comprised approximately two million of the thirty million people who populated 1910 Turkey. They were a despised minority.

But they had been there first. They were natives of the land, predating their oppressors by two and a half millennia.

The Armenians are one of the oldest civilizations of the Near East—a proud, industrious, and resilient people. Henry Morgenthau, the American Ambassador to Turkey during World War I and an outspoken defender of the Armenians during Turkey's atrocities against them, wrote of them with admiration:

---

[13] Dawn Anahid MacKeen, *The Hundred-Year Walk: An Armenian Odyssey* (New York: Houghton Mifflin Harcourt, 2016), 6.

[14] G. J. Meyer, *A World Undone* (New York: Delacorte Press-Random House, 2006), 334.

In the northeastern part of Asia Minor, bordering on Russia, there were six provinces in which Armenians formed the largest element in the population. From the time of Herodotus [fifth century BC] this portion of Asia has borne the name of Armenia. The Armenians of the present day are the direct descendants of the people who inhabited the country three thousand years ago. Their origin is so ancient that it is lost in fable and mystery. . . . What is definitely known about the Armenians, however, is that for ages they have constituted the most civilized and most industrious race in the eastern section of the Ottoman Empire. . . . Everywhere they are known for their industry, their intelligence, and their decent and orderly lives. They are so superior to the Turks intellectually and morally that much of the business and industry had passed into their hands.[15]

During that first drive with Dr. Panosian, I asked him if the term "Armenian" describes an ethnicity or a religion? The answer is *yes*. The Armenian people have inhabited the Near East for over three millennia. And for over half of that time, they have been a Christian people.

Ancient Armenia was the first country to declare Christianity as its national religion, doing so almost a century before the Roman Empire officially embraced Christianity. Panosian explains:

[Armenia's official turn to Christianity] was surely nominal: the king ordered his people to convert, and it did not mean universal conversion to Christ. But officially as a nation in 301 AD in response to the missionary work of one Gregory the Illuminator, the king Tirdat embraced Christianity and declared it to be the official religion of the nation.[16]

Nearly two millennia later, Armenians are also among the *last remaining* Middle Easterners to claim Christ. While the rest of the region succumbed to the Islam of the conquering Ottoman Empire beginning in the fifteenth century, Armenians held tenaciously to their Christian faith, though it has cost them dearly. Ambassador Morgenthau (himself a Jew) called the Armenians "a little island of Christians surrounded by backward peoples of hostile religion and hostile race."[17]

---

[15] Henry Morgenthau, *Ambassador Morgenthau's Story* (self-pub., CreateSpace, 2017), 194.

[16] Panosian, *Islam and the Bible*, 1.

[17] Morgenthau, *Ambassador Morgenthau's Story*, 194.

Because they are a religious minority in one of the world's most difficult places, the history of Armenian Christians is a bloody history. Francis Whiting Halsey described their plight vividly in 1919: "Since Noah's ark rested on Mount Ararat it is doubtful whether the inhabitants of those mountains have ever enjoyed any long spell of peace."[18] Over and over again, Armenians have gained religious freedom, only to face a new form of oppression and be forced to fight for liberty yet again. The patron saint of the Armenian church is Vardan Mamikonian (387–451), who fought the Persians at the Battle of Avaryar. Mamikonian lost his life in order to gain the religious freedom of Armenian Christians in his day. His story of tragedy and triumph for religious freedom is a microcosm of the history of his people.

In the late nineteenth and early twentieth centuries, Armenians were oppressed and systematically murdered by the Turks. While the suffering of the Armenians under their Muslim neighbors had gone on since the Ottomans' conquest of the region in the fifteenth century, it reached an especially savage level between 1895 and 1915, continuing without reprieve and climaxing in two ghastly events:

- In 1895, Turkish Sultan Abdul Hamid II was responsible for the slaying of two hundred thousand to three hundred thousand Armenians; he stopped only because he was threatened by Russia, Great Britain, and France. His role in the ethnic cleansing earned him the infamous nickname "the Bloody Sultan."
- In 1915, Abdul Hamid's plans to solve what Turks called "the Armenian problem" by exterminating the Armenians were revived by the very men who had deposed him— "the Young Turks" and, eventually, "the Three Pashas."[19] The brutality of these men was even worse than Hamid's. They

---

[18] Francis Whiting Halsey, *The Literary Digest History of the World War* (New York: Funk & Wagnalls, 1919), VIII: 34.

[19] "The Young Turks" were a reform group who deposed Hamid and promised to institute a constitutional government. At their ascendance, even Armenians anticipated a future of safety and security. However, the new government soon splintered into a power struggle, eventually won by Grand Vizier Talaat Pasha, who ruled alongside war minister Enver Pasha and naval minister Djemai Pasha—"the Three Pashas."

systematically killed almost one million Armenians in one bloody year.

In the twenty years between 1895 and 1915, more than one and a half million Armenians—75% of the Armenian population—were murdered by Turkish soldiers and citizens.[20] This great crime is remembered as "the Armenian Genocide," what historian John Buchan calls "one of the most wholesale and cold-blooded massacres" in history.[21]

The persecution of the Armenian people didn't begin or end with the genocide. Their suffering has been relentless. With the fall of the Ottoman Empire at the conclusion of World War I, Armenians were granted independence by the victorious Allies (Britain, France, and Italy). But tragically, those powers were so fatigued by The Great War that they failed to support the Armenian government they had helped to establish. The fledgling Armenian state was soon overrun by Turkish forces under the lead of Mustafa Kemal, affectionately known as "Atatürk," the founder of modern Turkey. Thus, the Armenians were suppressed again by the Turks, this time under a new name: the Republic of Turkey. To free themselves from the rule of the murderous Turks, they eventually submitted instead to a new oppressor: atheistic Communists from Russia following the Bolshevik Revolution of 1917. Under Communist rule, the religious persecution continued. Even in recent years, just to the south of modern Turkey, many of the Christians who were martyred by Saddam Hussein in Iraq's "religious cleansing" were ethnic Armenians. As Ambassador Morgenthau wrote almost a century ago, "Their long existence has been one unending martyrdom."[22]

Amazingly, in a turnabout like the Israelis' return to their homeland in 1948, the Armenian nation has finally regained independence in its own land, or at least a portion of its own land. After hundreds of years of a virtual exile on their own soil, the Republic of Armenia was

---

[20] In addition to 1.5 million Armenian Christians, the Turks killed hundreds of thousands of Assyrian and Chaldean Christians as well, and focused their post-war persecutions on Greek Christians, tens of thousands of whom were killed in 1922.

[21] John Buchan, *A History of the Great War* (Boston: Houghton Mifflin, 1922), II: 395.

[22] Morgenthau, *Ambassador Morgenthau's Story*, 194.

formed in 1991 with the dissolution of the Soviet Union. Modern Armenia is landlocked, bordered by Turkey on the west, Iran on the south, Azerbaijan on the east, and Georgia on the north. The population of modern Armenia is now around three million, 98% of whom are ethnic Armenians. Millions more have been scattered around the world—the Armenian *diaspora*.

The Armenian Apostolic Church is one of the Eastern Orthodox churches. In many ways, it is but one step away from Roman Catholicism. It is steeped in icons and works-based attempts to gain God's favor. "Incense, but no gospel," as Panosian puts it. But there are notable exceptions. There are priests who preach the gospel in the Armenian Apostolic Church. And there are families, like the Momjians and Panosians in this story, who have embraced the gospel by trusting in Jesus Christ alone. In fact, many of the western missionaries who went to Turkey to convert Muslims to Christianity in the late nineteenth and early twentieth centuries found that they had greater success evangelizing religious but lost Armenians instead.

Smpat Chorbadjian is one example of an Armenian who turned from the formalism of the Armenian church and was born again by faith in Jesus Christ. In his book *Surviving the Forgotten Armenian Genocide,* he tells of his escape from the Turks during World War I. He also tells of his escape from the guilt of his sins through his faith in Jesus Christ. Chorbadjian came to understand that he was unable to save himself from his sins. He needed a Savior. He shares the prayer which he offered at the time of his conversion:

> Lord Jesus, you know I'm a sinner, and if I die in my sins I will go to hell. But you are merciful, and I know if I come to You, You will not turn me away. Therefore, this morning I come to you, with all my sins. Forgive my sins, and after this, give me the strength to turn from my sins and help me. Amen.[23]

---

[23] Smpat Chorbadjian, *Surviving the Forgotten Armenian Genocide: A Moving Personal Story,* ed. Patrick Sookhdeo (McLean, VA: Isaac Publishing), 99.

His faith is the same faith of Ed and Betty Panosian. Dr. and Mrs. Panosian are born-again Christians. Though moral people in the eyes of the world, they know that they are guilty sinners in the eyes of God. Like Chorbadjian, they have repented of their sins and cried out to Jesus to do for them what they could not do for themselves—to save them. Since receiving Christ as their Savior, they have dedicated their lives to sharing the gospel with all who will hear, and it is fitting that this book should do the same. The hope of the sinner lies neither in his own good deeds nor in his association with any particular church.[24] The only Savior for sinners is Jesus Christ—alone.[25]

The Scriptures repeatedly speak of the Messiah as a "root" or "sprig" (Isaiah 4:2; Jeremiah 33:15; Zechariah 3:8–9; 6:12). It's a beautiful image. It pictures the stump of a fallen tree, which appears lifeless. With astounding resiliency, a sprig will often grow out of what seems to be a dead stump. The Messiah arose from the nation of Israel, though King David's royal line had apparently been cut off centuries before.

The sprig is a fitting symbol for the Armenians, as well. They have been cut off by countless oppressors. They have lost wars. They have gone into exile in other nations. They have existed as a despised minority, surrounded and suppressed by their enemies. In the wake of the Armenian Genocide, this people group appeared to be finished. Yet, they continue to exist. Just when the Armenian stump looks to be dead, a sprig emerges, and the stunning story of this heroic people continues.

---

[24] Ephesians 2:8–9 KJV: "For by grace are ye saved through faith; and that not of yourselves: it is the gift of God: Not of works, lest any man should boast."

[25] John 14:6 KJV: "Jesus saith unto him, 'I am the way, the truth, and the life: no man cometh unto the Father, but by me.'"

CHAPTER FOUR

A NATION TORN

THE PAST 2,000 YEARS — TURKEY

*"It is this circumstance which has given [Turkey]
a predominant factor in human history—the
function of a land-link between two continents."*

—Seton Lloyd[26]

Ed Panosian's Armenian ancestors hail from Turkey, a land of exquisite beauty and fascinating history.

Turkey (sometimes called *Anatolia*) is home to some of the finest ancient ruins in the world. Sites such as Perge, Aspendos, Aphrodisias, Hierapolis, Didyma, Pinara, Miletus, and Ephesus attract tourists from around the globe. Turkey has a wealth of marble columns, ancient agoras, and breathtaking gateways. Best preserved are the ancient theaters, which were built into hillsides and thus have survived relatively intact compared to free-standing structures. Turkey is a historian's paradise.

But its natural beauty may outdistance even its history. It boasts dramatic mountain ranges: the Taurus Mountains in the south (rugged mountains, through which the apostle Paul hiked on his tortuous missionary journeys), the Pontic Mountains in the north, and most impressively, the rugged Armenian Highlands in the east, part of the ancient kingdom of Armenia. With an elevation of almost 17,000 feet, Mount Ararat towers above them all.

Central Turkey holds one of the most unusual geographical sites of the entire world. Göreme National Park, near Cappadocia, almost

---

[26] Seton Lloyd, *Ancient Turkey: A Traveler's History* (Berkley: University of California Press, 1989), 13.

defies description. It is home to large, white, cone-shaped rock forma-
tions that stand erect, stretching out of the ground like fingers. Turks
whimsically call them "fairy chimneys." The stone is soft, and scores of
the enormous natural pillars were hollowed out and made into homes
and churches by Christians who fled to Göreme from their Roman
oppressors in the early centuries of the Christian church. Beautiful
frescos dating back to the tenth century are still visible in many of
these rugged chapels. If the astounding natural beauty weren't enough,
at sunrise modern Göreme is made even more magnificent by the
appearance of dozens of colorful hot-air balloons which dot the sky to
give tourists in the air and on the ground an unforgettable view.

Göreme looks like enormous white candles jutting toward the
sky; Pamukkale looks like those candles have melted and hardened
again into enormous white pools. For centuries, Pamukkale has drawn
crowds to its natural thermal baths. The white deposits of calcium and
the blue pools of water they hold appear almost too perfect to be real.

Turkey is beautiful—but it is also bountiful, thanks to its natural
resources and location. It is a major player in the modern oil market.
It served as a valuable ally for the United States during the latter half
of the twentieth century, housing American military bases near the
Soviet Union and at the edge of the powder keg that is the Middle
East. Its strategic location has given it economic and military prominence for millennia, not just in modern times.

To the east of modern Turkey lie Iran, Iraq, and Syria. To the west
and south, the Mediterranean Sea draws tourists to exotic beaches
and tropical islands. To the north lies the Black Sea, connected to the
Mediterranean only by Turkey's Bosphorus Strait and the Dardanelles,
giving Turkey one of the most economically strategic locations in the
world—the gateway between Northern Europe and Africa.[27] Procop-

---

[27] The importance of the Bosphorus Strait and the Dardanelles was shown in World War I.
By closing the Dardanelles in 1914, Germany isolated Russia from its allies, Great Britain and
France. Unable to gain ammunition, the massive Russian army was rendered useless, and Russia
was defeated only a year later. Germany manipulated Turkey into an alliance primarily to control
the waterway between Russia and the rest of the world.

ius (500–554 AD), the Byzantine historian, called the Bosphorus "the strait that surpasses all straits, because with one key it opens and closes two worlds, two seas."[28] The two seas are the Black Sea and the Aegean Sea, which also leads to the massive Mediterranean. The two worlds are Europe and Asia.[29]

Procopius saw the Bosphorus as a key that unlocked the West and the East, but the entire country of Turkey might also be compared to a rope. Turkey doesn't just connect Europe and Asia, the West and the East; it is pulled by them, back and forth, in a perpetual tug-of-war. Traveling from east to west in this country feels like traveling through time: from traditional living to modernity, from fundamental Islam to secularism and commercialism, from oppression to freedom. Turkey has tried in vain to gain acceptance into the European Union. But Turkey is more Asian than European. Historian Philip Jenkins concurs: "Traveling east from Istanbul means entering another culture, another history, and another civilization, and that Islamic dominance remains obvious as far east as Pakistan. In common perceptions, the Middle East is a Muslim East."[30]

Turkey has endured a perpetual identity crisis, both because of its location and its religious history. To introduce yet another metaphor, Turkey is a tree with pagan roots, a Christian trunk, and Islamic branches.

Scripture first speaks of the lands we know as Turkey way back in the book of Genesis, near the beginning of time. Mount Ararat, cited as the landing place of the ark in which God delivered Noah and his family, is in Turkey.[31] In later Old Testament times, Turkey was the home of the Hittites. In the last hundred years, archeological digs throughout central Turkey have unearthed many Hittite sites. The Hittites appear in Scripture primarily as the military enemies of

---

[28] Quoted in Freely, 5.
[29] In reality, Turkey is the meeting point of three continents: Europe, Asia, and Africa.
[30] Philip Jenkins, *The Great and Holy War: How World War I Became a Religious Crusade* (New York: Harper One, 2014), 288.
[31] Genesis 8:4.

Israel.[32] Of course, the most noteworthy Hittite in Scripture is Uriah, the husband of Bathsheba and the man murdered by King David.[33]

In New Testament times, the land we now call Turkey was the focal point of Christian expansion. It is home to Antioch (near modern-day Antakya), the metropolitan church that became the catapult for early Christian missions. In many ways, the church at Antioch surpassed even Jerusalem as the headquarters of the early Christian church.[34]

Central Turkey saw the first church plants of the apostle Paul's missionary journeys: Pisidian Antioch, Iconium, Derbe, and Lystra.[35] The seven churches of Revelation, to which Jesus (through the apostle John) wrote seven letters, are all in western Turkey: Ephesus, Smyrna, Pergamum, Thyatira, Sardis, Philadelphia, Laodicea.[36] The sites of all seven cities can be visited today, though not all contain equally compelling sights. By far the crown jewel of the seven churches is Ephesus, one of the great cities of the ancient world and one of the great churches of ancient Christianity. The ruins of the ancient city—including its exquisite library and remarkably well-preserved theater—attract almost two million visitors each year. Walking down an ancient road and looking into the grand theater, one can almost hear the echoes of the riot recorded in the book of Acts: "Great is Diana of the Ephesians!"[37]

Christian history in the region did not end with the closing of the canon of Scripture. The Nicene Creed, still recited today by Christians around the world, was penned there, at the Council of Nicaea in 325 AD. The cities of Nicaea, Constantinople, Ephesus, and Chalcedon were home to all of the Seven Ecumenical Councils of the fourth through eighth centuries, and all are located in modern-day Turkey. While Christianity was born in Jerusalem, it grew up in Turkey.

---

[32] Exodus 23:28; Joshua 1:4; *et al.*
[33] 2 Samuel 12:9–10.
[34] Acts 11:19–30; 13:1–3.
[35] Acts 14–15.
[36] Revelation 2–3.
[37] Acts 19:28, 34 KJV.

Although Turkey is home to cherished Christian sites, it is now a thoroughly Muslim country.[38] Islam is a permeating force, especially in the interior and the east. Turkey has tolerated Christians since the fall of Constantinople to the Ottomans in 1453, but with restrictions and, sometimes, persecutions. The Islam practiced in Turkey is moderate compared to some of Turkey's Middle Eastern neighbors, although it has become more radical even in the last decade. Proselytizing isn't expressly illegal, but Turkish Christians keep a low profile. Persecution continues.[39] Revelation's seven churches have been replaced by innumerable mosques.

———————

No city shows the European/Asian divide and Christian/Islamic divide of Turkey more than Istanbul, formerly Constantinople, one of the great cities of the world. It is a gorgeous city, beguiling and picturesque despite its massive size. Dawn Anahid MacKeen describes it as "beautiful Constantinople, with its seven hills, minarets, steeples, and boats that [bob] on cobalt waters."[40] Istanbul is the meeting place of east and west, of north and south, of history and modernity. It lies on prime real estate economically—literally sprawling onto the banks of two continents. But it is no less strategically located culturally and religiously. Outside of Jerusalem, no city has such a tumultuous religious heritage. Its tortuous history is best told using the city's successive names: Byzantium, Constantinople, and Istanbul.

Byzantium — According to legend, Byzantium was founded in the seventh century BC by Byzas, the leader of the Greek city of Megara. It was settled on the European side of the Bosphorus, though it later conquered Chalcedon on the Asiatic side and thereby gained

———————

[38] The Republic of Turkey was designed by Mustafa Kemal Atatürk to be a secular country politically. It is a Muslim country *religiously*—98% Muslim, in fact—and it has become more Muslim in its politics in recent years.

[39] At the time of writing, for example, an American Christian missionary was being held in a Turkish prison on seemingly spurious charges.

[40] MacKeen, *The Hundred-Year Walk,* 90.

control of shipping between the Black and Aegean Seas. Over the centuries, it was conquered and controlled by successive Empires: Persia in 513 BC, Greece in 411 BC, and finally Rome in 196 AD. Because of its strategic location, it continued to grow in prominence until the fourth century AD, when the decision of one man made it the most important city in the world.

Constantinople — The Roman Emperor Constantine was a remarkable and audacious man. Despite hundreds of years of official Roman persecution of Christians, Constantine legalized Christianity with the Edict of Milan in the year 313. He embraced the Christian faith himself, and he paved the way for Christianity to become the official religion of the Empire under Emperor Theodosis I's Edict of Thessalonica in 380. Constantine's protection and preference of Christianity was a remarkable turnabout, though it was certainly more political in nature than spiritual. One doesn't become a Christian by decree, but by true, repentant faith in Jesus Christ. But even if true *Christianity* wasn't embraced by Roman subjects—and it wasn't— *Christendom* as a cultural and political force was invented by Constantine.

Constantine had another audacious move to make. A decade after embracing Christianity, he moved the capital of the Roman Empire out of Rome. Think of that! Forsaking the city after which the Empire was named, he chose the ancient city of Byzantium as the seat of his government, relocating there in 324. He renamed Byzantium *Nova Roma*—New Rome, but just a few years later, in 330, it was again renamed, this time after its Emperor: Constantinople. It would be the capital of the Byzantine Empire for more than one thousand years, long after the Roman Empire to the west had fallen.

Istanbul — Constantinople, the "New Rome," reigned for a millennium. That's hard to imagine in our modern era. Even in the last one hundred years we have seen nations rise and fall as though they were disposable and maps become outdated as soon as their ink was dry. What a contrast to Constantinople! The great city seemed impregnable, despite the threat of the Ottomans who had swept across Asia like wildfire. But to the shock of the world, even this great city on the

Bosphorus was unable to withstand the young sultan, Mehmed II. My friend David Hosaflook, who has devoted his life to both the gospel and the history of the Near East, explains:

> [Europeans] considered Constantinople (Istanbul) an impenetrable buffer city to the East, as it had successfully resisted invading armies for more than a millennium. With Constantinople as its great wall and the Adriatic Sea as its great moat, Europe felt safe and remained focused on its internal disputes.
>
> In the spring of 1453, the world changed. In just fifty-four days a new Ottoman sultan managed to do the impossible: he besieged and defeated Constantinople, declared it his capital, converted its grand Hagia Sophia into a mosque, and took his seat upon the throne of the Caesars. With greater exploits in holy war than all previous Muslim sovereigns, it seemed obvious to him—if not divinely ordained—that he should become lord of the world. At only twenty-one years of age, he was Mehmed II *the Conqueror*.[41]

The Ottomans were now on the doorstep of Europe. They would eventually push into eastern Europe, capturing Greece and Hungary and very nearly overrunning the rest of Europe. In God's providence, they were stalled by an unlikely band of warriors—Albanians who, with the help of the Venetians, defended their homes and families in Shkodra and thereby defended the rest of Europe. These heroes resisted the irresistible, defying impossible odds and thwarting the sultan—ever infatuated with conquering Rome—by delaying his assault on the Italian Peninsula.

If no city shows the strain between Christianity and Islam like Istanbul, no single building shows the rivalry like the beautiful and ancient Hagia Sophia. The current building was originally built between the years 532 and 537—almost 1500 years ago! It is massive, and its dome is an amazing sight from both inside the basilica and from outside, where it can be seen for miles, towering above the city.

---

[41] David Hosaflook, editor's preface to *The Siege of Shkodra: Albania's Courageous Stand Against Ottoman Conquest, 1478,* (Tirana, Albania: Onufri Publishing House, 2012), xvii. *The Siege of Shkodra* is a classic piece of Albanian history written by Marin Barleti in 1504 and painstakingly edited and translated into English by Hosaflook. It is a fascinating read on the aggressive advance of the Ottoman Empire and the heroic opposition of the Albanians.

When Constantinople was conquered by the Ottomans in 1453, the church was turned into a mosque. Christian paintings and images were discarded or plastered over. Four minarets (signifying a mosque of the highest order) were erected. In 1935, the mosque was converted into a museum. But it is still distinctly Muslim, not Christian, in appearance.

The transformation of that ancient building is typical of the often-bloody transformation of the territories of the Ottoman Empire. At times Christians have been oppressed, removed, forcefully converted, and destroyed, like the Christian symbols of the great basilica. Persecution has not typically been official state policy. Turkey has a degree of religious freedom even today. But on many occasions Christian minorities like the Armenians were barely tolerated—until they weren't.

The ancient and the modern, the East and the West, the Christian and the Islamic—all meet in Turkey, like twenty pounds of produce stuffed into a ten-pound bag. Sometimes its seams have held. Sometimes they have torn. And sometimes the entire bag has been shredded, leaving devastation. The Turkish Armenian story is a story of tearing, shredding, and devastation.

The Hagia Sophia in Istanbul; photo by Greg Buckland, 2017

CHAPTER FIVE

AN EGG FOR TOBACCO

1901 — BALAN, TURKEY

". . . whose end is destruction, whose God is their belly,
and whose glory is in their shame . . ."

—Philippians 3:19

Nazar Panosian carefully made his way through the dirt roads of his hometown—Balan, Turkey.[42] He carried in his cupped hands an egg—the last egg in his family's possession. He had been sent by his father to sell it and purchase some tobacco.

In the words of Ed Panosian, Nazar's father was "a godless man married to a godly woman." When his first son was born on November 11, 1893, he had named him after Nazareth, the village of Jesus' childhood, deferring to his wife, a devout Christian. But that was as far as his Christianity went. He was impatient with his wife, and her perpetual illness stirred his anger, not his pity. His treatment of his two sons alternated between disinterested passivity and cruelty.

Nazar moved quietly through the streets, passing fellow Armenians and coming under the glare of disapproving Turks. Even as his hands sheltered their precious cargo, his stomach must have rolled and groaned, and his mind must have devoured it—multiple times and in delectable ways: he could eat it boiled, his fingers carefully separating the yolk from its white casement. Or he could eat it fried and allow the yolk to seep down his chin. Even sucking it raw from its shell must have been tempting.

---

[42] Nazar's hometown of Balan also appears as *Beilan* in some resources.

What he should be doing, he rued, is feeding it to his mother. He was only nine years old, but already the injustice and selfishness of his father galled him. Nazar had an innate and unbending sense of right and wrong, and he knew this was wrong. His mother languished in bed, weak and malnourished. He and his five-year-old brother Manuel suffered hunger pangs. Yet his father insisted on trading food for tobacco, as if the stinking smoke could fill his family's bellies.

Still, he trudged dutifully through the streets, ignoring his grumbling stomach. Balan was a rural town on the eastern outskirts of Turkey, far from the bustle of Istanbul. Balan was far from *everything*, and it appeared in the year 1902 much as it had a hundred or even a thousand years before. Although much of the world was advancing with automobiles, telephones, and electricity, Balan knew little of the luxury of the newborn twentieth century.

Nazar and his Armenian friends and family were an ethnic and religious minority. For centuries, Islamic Turks had looked on the Armenians with contempt. Sometimes that contempt took the form of segregation. Always it took the form of bullying. Occasionally it boiled over into murderous riots. That was life for Armenians—their miserable but unavoidable "normal." They lived with a permanent dread. Their homeland, if you could call it that, was hostile, and it had been ever since the Ottomans overran the Middle and Near East in the fifteenth century.

Having sold the egg, Nazar approached the tobacco shop. He could smell its stale smoke from over a block away. Nazar walked in and immediately felt the disapproving gaze of the shop owner, a Muslim. The man did not shoo him away; Muslims weren't so prejudiced they'd turn away business. But he didn't welcome him either. Rather than hurrying over to his young Armenian customer, he kept the boy waiting.

Nazar's eyes and throat burned from the smoke, and he was eager to get the tobacco in hand and make his escape. The smoke was starting to nauseate him. He let out a small cough, which amused the shop owner. Finally, as though satisfied that the boy had suffered sufficiently, the man sauntered over, took his money, and handed over the tobacco with a dismissive jerk of his head.

Nazar was relieved to be back in the street. His lungs drank in the fresh air. He was unsure what was more suffocating—the smoke or the contempt he had felt from the man. The hatred exchanged between Turks and Armenians was ubiquitous in Balan as it was throughout Turkey, and Nazar felt it keenly. Perhaps avoiding such an unpleasant experience is what prompted Nazar's father to send his son on the errand instead of going himself.

Nazar snaked back through Balan's narrow streets, cradling the tobacco in his hands, just as he had the egg. He knew it was silly to be so cautious. Tobacco couldn't crack or break. Yet, he instinctively handled it with unreasonable care lest he should somehow provoke his father. He finally arrived home, relieved that his mission had been successful. Without speaking a word or even looking his father in the eyes, he unburdened himself of the tobacco. His stomach growled a final protest about the egg. His father took the tobacco and prepared to smoke it. He offered no greeting or word of thanks. But he gave no reproof either. Nazar let out a sigh of relief.

Nazar moved noiselessly across the dirt floor to his mother's bed-side, determined not to wake her. She was as kind as his father was harsh. *Godly*—that's what she was. That's how the women at church described her. Yet, she was fading. This he knew, despite his youth. And so he determined to enjoy her for as long as he could—to watch her, touch her, almost inhale her. He could not have explained it, but it was as though he knew he needed to absorb enough of her now to last him a lifetime.

Inevitably, as quiet as he tried to be, his mother would awaken under his gaze. She would look on him with tired but smiling eyes. He knew that she loved him. He knew that she wanted him to grow into an honest man—a *godly* man, not like his father, though she would never have disparaged her husband. She wanted Nazar to take care of his younger brother, Manuel. She wanted him to be strong enough for all of them, even if she could not be. Because she could not be.

Nazar's mother would not see his tenth birthday.

CHAPTER SIX

DRIED FRUIT AND ARMENIAN CIGARS

1910 — ANTAKYA, TURKEY

*"All the Armenians desired was security
for life, honour, and property."*

—Sir Edward Pears[43]

Less than one hundred miles from Nazar Panosian's village of Balan lies the ancient village of Antakya. The English name for Antakya is Antioch, and it has a storied past. It was the site of the first Christian church among the Gentiles. It was pastored by Barnabas, and eventually by the apostle Paul.[44] It was a multi-ethnic city in New Testament times, and even in modern times it is more diverse than most Turkish cities, due in part to its proximity to the border of Syria. Beyond being the first church plant among the Gentiles, Antioch became the launching pad from which Paul and Barnabas (and later, Paul and Silas) would depart on missionary journeys that took them all over Turkey and Greece.[45] Sadly, Christians in Antakya have been persecuted by Muslims for centuries, and the persecution continues today.

Christians and Muslims lived near each other in Antakya at the start of the twentieth century, but there was perpetual friction. Muslims could take advantage of Christians with impunity throughout Turkey, but the condition of Christians worsened the farther east you

---

[43] Sir Edwin Pears, a British journalist who lived in Istanbul; quoted in Peter Balakian, *The Burning Tigris*, 5.
[44] Acts 11:19–30.
[45] Acts 13–20.

traveled. Antakya was at the eastern extremity of the nation. To be sure, there were Muslims who maintained kind relations with their Christian neighbors, but they were the exception rather than the rule.

Antakya was the hometown of Ed Panosian's mother, Sara Momjian.

Sara was born to Sarkis and Emma Momjian in 1902. She was the second of four children, each separated by two years: James was the eldest, followed by Sara, Rose, and Mihran.[46]

Sarkis and Emma enjoyed a close, committed relationship. Their affectionate bond set the example for their children, who were also devoted to one another. Life was intolerably difficult for the Momjian family and for all Turkish Armenians. The sultan passed laws that not only tolerated but encouraged their mistreatment. National taxes were higher for them than for their Muslim neighbors, and a suffocating regional tax—essentially extortion money paid to local leaders—was intended to keep Armenians poor. It didn't work. Armenians were among the most successful citizens in Turkey, despite the discrimination they endured. The Momjians worked hard and enjoyed the fruits of their labors. Their Muslim neighbors admired and envied them, despite themselves.

Survival in such adverse conditions required everyone to pitch in. Even when Sara was only eight years old, she and her two younger siblings would help with household chores. James, her older brother, contributed as well as he could. He suffered from tuberculosis, and even slight exertion brought on violent coughing fits. Even this burden helped unite the family. Everyone did his part, and everyone did a little extra to help James.

Among the children's most important jobs was stringing fruits and vegetables. They would fill a string with fresh produce, then suspend it from the ceiling so it would dehydrate and be preserved for the winter. Armenians were excellent jewelers, craftsmen, and merchants,

---

[46] Ed Panosian's middle name is Miran, in honor of his mother's brother. The slight alteration in spelling is intentional.

but regardless of a father's career, *everyone* was a gardener, including children. Harvesting and drying fruits and vegetables was a task well suited to young children. Sara's home and hands often had the sweet aroma of figs, apricots, and dates.

Like every Armenian mother, Emma Momjian taught her girls to prepare Armenian dishes, sharing recipes that had been passed down for generations. The favorite dish of Sara's was *sarma,* or "Armenian cigars." The girls would help their mother mix rice, tomatoes, and meat with salt, pepper, and parsley. This mixture would be rolled into grape leaves, with the end product looking very like cigars. They would layer the edible cigars in a pan, cover them with sauce, and let it all simmer. The smell tormented them until their father arrived home and they could all enjoy eating together. Other cultures have their stuffed cabbage, but Armenians swear by their grape-leaf cigars!

Winters were long, and Sarkis Momjian heated his home with coal. Inside the house was a wooden coal bin, large enough for the children to hide in when it was not full. They would occasionally tuck themselves into the enormous box, delighting to jump out and frighten their unsuspecting siblings. Even their parents could be surprised—or at least feign being surprised. The cold winters brought Sara's favorite time of year: Christmas. She knew it was a holiday which her Muslim neighbors found annoying or even offensive. In a curious way, that made it even more special. Christmas embodied much of the Armenian existence in a hostile land. It was *their* holiday, celebrating *their* beliefs, and expressing *their* hopes and joys. They would be respectful when their neighbors observed Ramadan, but they would exult in their own celebration of Christmas.

Each member of the family could expect one Christmas gift. Initially, the gifts were chosen by their parents, but eventually the children were allowed to conspire about each other's presents. The gift might be a simple doll, or a brush, or a scarf. Nothing too costly. But it almost didn't matter what it was. It was *something,* and it was an expression of love. Someone had cared enough to prepare and wrap a present, and that was a wonderful feeling.

Emma (pregnant with Sara), Sarkis, and James Momjian, 1901

Family Christmas traditions climaxed in the delightful Christmas services they would enjoy with their Armenian church. Sarkis had a booming tenor voice. Panosian explains: "My grandfather, Sarkis, was a cantor—a singer in the Armenian evangelical church." The songs Armenians use in worship are hauntingly beautiful. The cantor's voice skillfully rises and falls in a chant-like sound, accentuated by the vocal tremors that are so distinctive of eastern cultures. The sound is somber, even mournful, befitting a people with a history of persecution and martyrdom. Armenians of Sara's childhood knew how to lament. The congregation would join at times, but they would also listen in rapt silence, and Sarkis' powerful voice would echo off the walls of their church building.

The hymns in the Momjians' church were distinctly Christian and distinctly Armenian. For Armenians, a small band of Christians gathering to worship and encourage one another amidst the antagonistic Muslim majority of Turkey was a lifeline. They had no *adhan* to call them to prayer as the Muslims did, five times throughout the day. But they had beautiful hymns. They had joy. And unlike their neighbors, they had Jesus.

While every Armenian family was at least nominally Christian, the Momjians were deeply committed to Christ. They would sing hymns together in their home. They would read Scripture together. They would pray together. And while Sara and her siblings lay in bed, they would hear their mother praying for them, almost as a nightly ritual—a practice Sara would continue when she had her own family. There was something deeply soothing about hearing the fervent cadence of her mother's prayers, even as she dozed off.

CHAPTER SEVEN

SHOES, GLORIOUS SHOES

1903 — BALAN, TURKEY

*"Walk into almost any shoe repair store and it's like
stepping back in time with the smells of polish, glue
and leather, and shelves of worn shoes that call to
mind a cobbler shop from another century."*

—Kimberly Fornek[47]

Nazar's father remarried with distasteful haste. His new bride was younger, and perhaps predictably, she wanted her own children, not hand-me-downs. She wanted nothing to do with the boys, especially Nazar. She tolerated him for a time, but within a few months, her new husband was looking for an apprenticeship for the boy. The fact that he eventually settled on a Muslim shoemaker in another village revealed how eager Nazar's father was to be rid of the boy, or at least to put an end to his new wife's complaints.

Nazar was ambivalent when he heard he would be leaving his home to become a cobbler's apprentice. Since his mother's death, his house was filled with painful memories. He didn't mind parting with the house, his father, or his stepmother. But he ached for his brother Manny and hated the thought of leaving him. And he regretted that he would have to leave school. He had finished only the third grade, and he was certain he would never return to the classroom. He never did.

---

[47] Kimberly Fornek, "Shoe Repair Shops Branch Out to Stay in Business," *The Chicago Tribune,* Dec. 19, 2016.

Nazar's departure was a cruel blow for Manny. Less than a year earlier he had lost his mother. Now he was losing his older brother, and in some ways, the only true family he had left. He wished he were going, too. Nazar cupped Manny's face in his hands. He gazed at him until their eyes locked, and he whispered to him: "Little brother, I will be back for you."

With that, Nazar left the only home he had ever known. Manny watched with a disconnected stillness. Adults worry about children who cry. If a child has an accident—say if he falls and hits his head—his bellows bring wide-eyed parents running to see what's wrong. But the truth is, the child who hits his head and makes no sound is in far worse danger. Crying is healthy. Crying is natural. Silence after a traumatic fall means something is wrong or broken.

Manny's big brother Nazar was entering a new world. But Manny himself was being left behind. He took it quietly, like he had been broken.

––––––––––

Nazar must have wondered what living with a Muslim master would be like. Imagine the anxiety of such a young boy facing such a massive change. In his young mind, every Turk must be as rude and hateful as the tobacco shop owner. As usual, his father offered no counsel, no encouragement, no small talk. They just walked.

They left the Armenian portion of Balan, then passed out of Balan altogether. They walked for almost an hour before reaching the next village. Nazar had never been so far from home. Though they did business together, Turks and Armenians lived segregated lives, huddling with their own kind as much as they could. Now, everywhere he looked he saw only Turks. Turkish men wore a *fez*—a rimless hat, usually made of felt, which clearly distinguished them from Armenians. The only Armenian in sight was his father, who seemed as uncomfortable as Nazar was. He saw no churches, only mosques. There were farms, homes, and businesses, but it was still foreign to everything Nazar had known. The walk of one hour had brought him to an entirely different world. He may as well have crossed an ocean.

They arrived at the shoe shop. Nazar was immediately aware of the pungent smell that wafted from the shop's doorway. If you've ever been in a shoe repair shop, you can never forget the aroma. Leather, glue, and shoe polish all mingle together to create one stout, almost intoxicating scent. There's nothing in the world quite like it. The sense of foreboding that had dogged Nazar for the entire journey dissipated, replaced by a voracious curiosity. He found the new smell to be absolutely delicious. The smoke in the tobacco shop had nauseated him. But this—*this* was exhilarating!

His eyes devoured the shop. Shoes of all kinds neatly lined the walls, two by two, as if preparing to parade to Ararat and the ark. Here he saw large piles of leather. There he saw piles of tiny nails, next to heels of various sizes. Over there he saw leather that had been cut into oddly shaped pieces: tongues, quarters, toe caps, and soles. Finally, his eyes fell on the workbench, where he was immediately drawn to tools he'd never seen before: several kinds of giant scissors, small hammers, leather punches of all sizes, a variety of files, and foot-shaped pieces of wood (called *lasts,* as he would later learn) around which the shoes were sewn. He had never even considered that shoes were *made* somewhere. And now he would learn how to turn all these seemingly random pieces of leather into beautiful shoes!

Already, he was eager to learn—driven to be the best apprentice and eventually the best cobbler the world had ever seen. He smiled, and he knew he would never be the same.

Nazar heard the voice of the cobbler, breaking the spell the shop had cast over him. This man could make his life miserable. Since he was a Muslim, he probably would, Nazar assumed. And yet, he seemed different from most men Nazar had encountered. His apron was dirty, and his hands were stained, but seemed to be the kind of "dirty" that comes from work rather than carelessness.

Nazar's father spoke with the cobbler in hushed tones. Standing beside the man wasn't particularly flattering to Mr. Panosian, who looked haggard and unkempt compared to the shoemaker. Whatever they discussed, Nazar's father didn't seem too concerned about his son's future. Perhaps the cobbler paid Mr. Panosian for the boy's services, making Nazar feel like an egg that had been traded for tobacco.

His father approached him, looked down his strong Armenian nose at him, and muttered something about not shaming the family. Moments later, he was gone, leaving Nazar with a strange man in a strange shop in a strange town.

———

Despite Nazar's prejudices, he found his master to be remarkably kind. Though he was focused on his business, he treated Nazar with respect. He dismantled many of the young boy's learned assumptions. Not all Armenians were good, as his father and stepmother had proven. And not all Turks were hateful, as his new master daily demonstrated. The first true mentor in his life was a kind Muslim. Nazar was confounded and delighted.

Nazar was nine years old when he began learning the shoe business. He had had no choice regarding his future profession, but he couldn't have been more pleased with his prospects. Turkey was intent on becoming modern, and modernity meant shoes. Nazar was learning a trade whose time had come.

Still, despite his enthusiasm, the beginning of his new profession was inglorious. Dr. Panosian explains:

> My father learned the trade from the bottom up. By that I mean that he learned first to tan cowhides. He would talk to us about walking barefoot in winter to the town well to draw water with which to tan the hides. He remembered being cold and freezing in the winter. He learned from the master shoemaker to make shoes in a day when only the wealthy could afford shoes. He was barefoot. I don't know when he started wearing shoes. But his children never were barefoot.[48]

———

[48] This statement was made through an emotional, reminiscent laugh. During the discussion about shoes, Dr. Panosian pointed out that he had only leather shoes as a child—"never tennis shoes." I thought I caught a bit of disdain when he said this, and I did my best to conceal my tennis shoes from his line of vision.

Nazar was a quick learner and a hard worker. He learned to manufacture and repair shoes, all by hand. He worked hard to please even the rudest customers, many of whom probably expected much less from "an infidel." The cobbler knew Nazar Panosian wouldn't be an apprentice for long. He generously poured himself into the boy. The Muslim man taught the Christian boy to make shoes. He taught him how to run a business. He taught him how to work hard to make a living, and to do so without cheating his customers. More than that, he taught him how to treat people—even people different from himself. Every single one of the lessons took.

Nazar's childhood was over. He was a working man, as young as he was. His life was all about shoes—as it would be for the next seventy years.

PART THREE

"THROUGH THE VALLEY OF THE SHADOW OF DEATH"

CHAPTER EIGHT

THE SCOURGE BEGINS

1894–1896 — SMALL VILLAGES
IN EASTERN TURKEY

*"We must understand the basic fact underlying the Turkish
mentality is its utter contempt for all other races. . . . The
common term applied by the Turk to the Christian is 'dog,'
and in his estimation this is no mere rhetorical figure; he
actually looks upon his European neighbours as far less
worthy of consideration than his own domestic animals."*

—United States Ambassador Henry Morgenthau[49]

In 303 AD, the persecution of Christians became the official policy of the Roman Empire. The Emperor Diocletian published four
edicts which led to the greatest persecution of believers in the history
of the Empire—and, ironically, to the unprecedented growth of the
Christian faith.[50]

Diocletian made opposition to Christianity official. But the persecution of Christians by Roman rulers predated Diocletian's edicts by
over two centuries. The Emperor Nero is infamous for his slaughter
of Christians in the first century. Those martyred under Nero's scep-
ter include the apostles Paul and Peter. Persecution was *practiced* long
before it was *policy*.

So it is with the Turks' murder of the Armenians. Armenians recognize April 24, 1915, as the beginning of the genocide. And in a

---

[49] Morgenthau, *Ambassador Morgenthau's Story*, 187.
[50] As Tertullian famously declared, "The blood of the martyrs is the seed of the church."

way, it was. The arrest, deportation, and eventual murder of prominent Armenian citizens on that dark day mark the start of the bloodiest year of the Armenians' persecution. *One million Armenians were killed in 1915.* But the murder of Armenians didn't commence in 1915—it crescendoed. The bloodshed began in earnest twenty years earlier.

Sultan Abdul Hamid II ruled the Ottoman Empire from 1876 to 1909. To return to the Roman analogy, Hamid is the "Nero" of the Armenian tragedy. It was Hamid who was in power in the 1890s when the persecution of Armenians escalated from isolated murders to a sweeping ambition.

Once the strongest regime in the world and a threat which very nearly spilled into Western Europe, the Ottoman Empire tottered on the verge of collapse by the time of Hamid's rule, earning the infamous nickname "the Sick Man of Europe." The economy was a wreck. Poverty was rampant. Government corruption was unchecked, starting with the maniacal sultan. Turkey's many humiliations created two great hungers: (1) for the Turkish majority to flex its collective muscles, and (2) for someone to serve as a scapegoat for the failing empire. The Armenian minority was a convenient victim that served both purposes.

British Prime Minister William Ewart Gladstone dubbed Hamid "the Bloody Sultan" and "the Great Assassin." In the late nineteenth century Hamid's Turkey faced what would become known as "The Armenian Question"—a debate over how the country should handle its minority Christian subjects. Only the sultan had any real authority to address the question, and his answer was, utter annihilation.

Hamid began by suppressing mention of Armenians in books and newspapers. He imprisoned Armenian teachers. He essentially pretended the Armenians didn't exist, and then began to work to turn his fantasy of a world without Armenians into reality. Between 1894 and 1896, he ordered both soldiers and vigilantes to slaughter Armenian Christians. He promised eternal rewards to Muslims who carried out his murderous orders. And there were countless Muslims who did. The Turks' murder of the Armenians under Abdul Hamid is shocking not only for the staggering number of victims—between 200,000 and 300,000—but for the killers' utter savagery. Dissatisfied with merely killing their Armenian victims, Turkish Muslims tortured and slaughtered them in gruesome, sadistic ways.

American missionary Frederick Davis Greene's book *The Armenian Crisis in Turkey* contains graphic eyewitness accounts of the slaughters of 1894.[51] The testimonials he collected and presents as "letters," in a chapter aptly titled "A Chapter of Horrors," are difficult to read, but a small sampling is necessary to understand the atrocities suffered by Armenians.

From letter 5:

A lot of women, variously estimated from 60 to 160 in number, were shut up in a church, and the soldiers were "let loose" among them. Many of them were outraged [raped] to death, and the remainder dispatched with sword and bayonet. A lot of young women were collected as spoils of war. . . . Children were placed in a row, one behind another, and a bullet fired down the line, apparently to see how many could be dispatched with one bullet. Infants and small children were piled one on the other and their heads struck off.[52]

From letter 7:

No respect was shown to age or sex. Men, women, and infants were treated alike except that the women were subjected to greater outrage [rape] before they were slaughtered. . . . In one place three or four hundred women, after being forced to serve the vile purposes of

[51] Josiah Strong wrote of Greene's impeccable credentials in the introduction to Greene's book: "The author is thoroughly equipped for his task. Birth, residence, and travel in Turkey have made him personally acquainted with the situation which he discusses, and the independence of his position enables him to write without restraint and without prejudice. After nearly four years of service as a missionary of the American Board in Van, the centre of Armenia, during which no criticism of his course was ever made either by the Board or by the Turkish Government, he was recently ordered by his physician to return to America. Having resigned his connection with the American Board, he writes as the representative of no society, religious or political, and is connected with none. In issuing this book he is simply discharging what to him is a personal and unavoidable obligation; and as he frankly avows its authorship, it will be impossible for the Turkish Government to hold any one else responsible for it." Frederick Davis Greene, *The Armenian Crisis in Turkey: The Massacre of 1894, Its Antecedents and Significance* (New York: Knickerbocker Press, 1895), v.
[52] Greene, *The Armenian Crisis in Turkey,* 14.

merciless soldiery, were taken to a valley nearby and hacked to pieces with sword and bayonet.[53]

From letter 8:

Women were outraged [raped] and then butchered; a priest taken to the roof of his church and hacked to pieces; young men piled in with wood saturated with kerosene and set on fire; a large number of women and girls collected in a church, kept for days, violated by the brutal soldiers, and then murdered. It is said that the number was so large that blood flowed from the church door.[54]

Grigoris Balakian records similar terrors with horrid redundancy in his book *Armenian Golgotha*. One example will suffice:

When they reached the area under the bridge, police and police soldiers, having joined the savage mob, set upon these poor, defenseless women—mothers, brides, virgins—and children. Just as spring trees are cut down with bill-hooked hedge knives, the bloodthirsty mob attacked this group of more than four hundred with axes, hatchets, shovels, and pitchforks, hacking off their appendages: noses, ears, legs, arms, fingers, shoulders. . . . They dashed the little children against the rocks before the eyes of their mothers while shouting, "Allah, Allah."[55]

Hamid wasn't able to see his evil plan through to completion. The butchery of 1894–1896 was stalled by the objections of neighboring nations, including France, Great Britain, and Russia. But while the murder of multitudes was slowed for a time, it did not stop. Hamid's diabolical answer to the Armenian Question spilled into the twentieth century, one village at a time, until the downpour of death became an absolute deluge in 1915. In the words of historian Philip Jenkins, Hamid's atrocities served as "a dress rehearsal for the later genocide."[56]

Patrick Sookhdeo tells how this bloody history is the story of all Armenians.

---

[53] Greene, *The Armenian Crisis in Turkey*, 26.
[54] Greene, *The Armenian Crisis in Turkey*, 28.
[55] Grigoris Balakian, *Armenian Golgotha*, 88.
[56] Jenkins, *The Great and Holy War*, 293.

Every Armenian family I have ever met carries a sorrow that has burdened them for a hundred years—the tragedy of the lost generations who suffered and died in what Armenians call their "Golgotha."[57]

"Every Armenian family"—including Ed Panosian's.

---

[57] Patrick Sookhdeo, foreword to *Surviving the Forgotten Armenian Genocide: A Moving Personal Story* (McLean, VA: Isaac Publishing), vii.

CHAPTER NINE

"DEATH TO THE INFIDELS"

1910 — ANTAKYA, TURKEY

*"Turkish rule . . . meant unutterable contempt. . . . The
Armenians (and the Greeks) were dogs and pigs . . . to be spat
upon, if their shadow darkened a Turk, to be outraged, to be the
mats on which he wiped the mud from his feet. Conceive the
inevitable result of centuries of slavery, of subjection to insult
and scorn, centuries in which nothing that belonged to the
Armenian, neither his property, his house, his life, his person,
nor his family, was sacred or safe from violence—capricious,
unprovoked violence—to resist which by violence meant death."*

—British Archeologist William Ramsay[58]

"There was no brutality they did not commit."

—Historian Francis Whiting Halsey[59]

In the year 1896, Hamid was forced by European powers to
retard his aggressive plan of Armenian extermination. However,
sporadic massacres continued for the next twenty years, unhindered
and unpunished. Ottoman Turks' first taste of Armenian blood made
them want more, not less. American Ambassador Henry Morgenthau
described the appalling plight of Armenians even in the years between
the bloodbaths of the mid-1890s and 1915:

---

[58] William Ramsay, the famous British archeologist and ethnographer, spent years in Turkey doing studies of biblical sites. William Ramsay, *Impressions of Turkey During Twelve Years' Wanderings* (London: Hodder & Stoughton-Aberdeen University Press, 1897), 206–207.
[59] Halsey, *The Literary Digest History of the World War,* VIII:50.

Abdul Hamid had to abandon his satanic enterprise of destroying a whole race by murder, yet Armenia continued to suffer the slow agony of pitiless persecution. Up to the outbreak of the European War, not a day had passed in the Armenian vilayets [provinces] without its outrages and its murders.[60]

Armenians in the Ottoman Empire lived in a virtual lions' den, never certain when the beasts who surrounded them would finally pounce. The massacres came to Antakya in the fall of 1910. One fateful day changed forever the lives of countless Armenians, including Ed Panosian's grandparents, Sarkis and Emma Momjian, and their four children.

The Momjians were in their home, going about their normal tasks. Without so much as a warning, a mob of Muslims, led by the sultan's Kurdish mercenaries, went on a parade of violence through Antakya, wreaking havoc on their Armenian neighbors. They fed their own rage, screaming themselves hoarse in the frenzy. They cursed the hated Armenian infidels, and they shouted praises to Allah: *"Allahu Akbar! Allahu Akbar!* Allah is the greatest! Allah is the greatest!" All the while they brutalized men, women, and children, allegedly at Allah's bidding.

The soldiers burst into the Momjian home, scattering furniture and breaking dishes. They thrust Emma and the children aside and focused their rage on Sarkis. Against so many, he was powerless to protect himself or his family. His children cowered in the corners of their small home, terror stricken. Despite his own frailty, James ran to his father's aid and tried to shield him. His attempt was pointless—and costly. He was knocked to the ground and kicked into the corner. His body lay motionless.

The invasion of the Momjian home ended suddenly and tragically. Dr. Panosian tells of his grandfather's tragic end: "They shot him in front of his wife and children. I can only imagine their reaction."

Sarkis Momjian, like countless thousands of his countrymen, had been murdered in his own home. His crime was two-fold: being an Armenian instead of a Turk and trusting in Jesus instead of Allah.

---

[60] Morgenthau, *Ambassador Morgenthau's Story*, 196.

Panosian describes one "bit of humanity in the midst of inhuman cruelty." Emma Momjian was pregnant at the time of her husband's murder. She herself was very nearly killed. Panosian retells the story as it was passed on to him:

> My grandmother, my mother's mother, was very evidently pregnant; and one of the Turkish soldiers said to the other, "Let's rip her open and see if it is a boy." They did not. The other soldier replied, "Have you no fear of Allah?"—that would have been going too far. They had just murdered my grandfather, but that would have been going too far.[61]

The murderers moved on to the next house. The Momjian home was sickeningly still. Emma and Sara wept quietly, muffling their sobs and their fears. The youngest children wailed. James lay in a heap on the ground, not yet moving. Sarkis would never move again.

How long they sat in traumatized terror is unknown. Emma went to nurse her wounded son, who could now add broken ribs and a collapsed lung to his tuberculosis. She was relieved to find that he was still alive.

She summoned a deep and previously unknown strength, even in her first moments as a widow and single mother. She quieted the children, first with words of kindness, then with a voice of command that startled even herself. She ordered them to prepare for the mob's return. Panosian picks up the story:

> In the midst of the weeping, after the murder of my grandfather, my grandmother ordered the children into the coal bin to hide and warned them against making any noise. "Don't sneeze! Don't talk! The soldiers may come back to get our food. Don't let them know you are there!" My mother said it was so stifling and confined, and there was coal dust. She had to hold her nose to keep from sneezing.

Emma knew they would be unable to stay in their home any longer, and yet she was unwilling to take the children out into the village

---

[61] Panosian, *Islam and the Bible*, 2.

until she was sure the violence had passed. She feared that she and her young daughters would be raped, a tragically common experience for defenseless Armenian women. After hiding her children in the coal bin, she ventured out by herself to find a place of refuge for her now fatherless family. She prayed that her home and her children would be left alone, but she had an ominous feeling that they would not.

Her fears were prescient. Her enemies retraced their steps and once again burst into the Momjian home. Stepping over Sarkis' dead body, they pillaged his home. The children listened from the coal bin, too terrified to even breathe. Sara was certain that at any moment she and her siblings would be discovered and killed.

The men took the items they wanted and broke the items they didn't.

One blessing of that unspeakably cruel day is that the soldiers, for whatever reason, wanted only provisions. They didn't see the children in the coal bin. They collected whatever food they could find, including the dried fruits and vegetables that still hung from the ceiling. They were infuriatingly efficient, and they left nothing behind. Sara, peering through slats in the coal bin, wanted to scream, "You can't take that! We've prepared it for months! We'll starve without it!" But her fear overcame her rage, and she only watched, mutely.

As quickly as they had come, the barbarians left. They had stolen the family's provisions. They had stolen their father. They had stolen their childhood and their innocence.

CHAPTER TEN

"THE STARVING ARMENIANS"

1910 — ANTAKYA, TURKEY

"What is to be done with the great mass of widows? . . .
All have children, without a father to support them."

—an unnamed missionary[62]

The Armenians weren't entirely friendless. There were contemporaries of the slaughter who objected to it and sought to intervene. The most notable among them was the American Ambassador to Turkey, Henry Morgenthau. An eyewitness of the devastation of 1915, he leveraged every ounce of influence at his disposal to end the atrocities against the Armenians. He acted heroically, though unsuccessfully. He is remembered today as a champion of the Armenian cause.

Another and earlier hero—or rather, heroine—was Clara Barton, the Good Samaritan of the Civil War and the founder of the Red Cross. At the age of eighty-five, Barton became the face of humanitarian efforts in Armenia, rallying for help in the United States and journeying to Istanbul from Boston in 1896.

Still another champion of the Armenians was a German evangelical leader named Johannes Lepsius. Dr. Lepsius begged Turkish leaders to extend mercy to the Armenians. When his pleas fell on deaf ears, he worked in secret to evacuate as many fellow Christians as he could, and to at least feed the ones whom he could not. All the while, he wrote courageously, exposing the Turks' treacheries to the world.

---

[62] A letter from a missionary in Armenia, published by J. Rendel Harris and Helen B. Harris, *Letters from the Scenes of the Recent Massacres in Armenia* (New York: Fleming H. Revell, 1897), 66.

Other friends of the Armenians were anonymous, but no less heroic. Christian missionaries scattered throughout Turkey were the "first responders" to the Armenian crisis, and they raised international awareness as they gave eyewitness reports of the persecution of Armenians. A handful of doctors did amazing work to heal the wounded and stop the spread of communicable diseases. Newspaper reporters sent dispatches to the West, often by transatlantic telegraph. Those sympathetic with "the starving Armenians" started societies and held rallies in the United States. Humanitarian and mission agencies campaigned for funds to help Armenian orphans, providing relief that saved the lives of thousands. On a lighter note, American children who were reluctant to eat their vegetables at the turn of the twentieth century were goaded into it by being told to "think of the starving Armenians!" Panosian quips, "Most of these American children would have been happy for the Armenians to have whatever it was!"

A world away, Emma Momjian and her children fit the description: they were starving Armenians, or at least in danger of starvation. Panosian comments, "The Turks did their evil and then left. The children and the widows fended for themselves."

Turkey had become too dangerous for Emma and her children. Sarkis' murder was one of thousands, and she was certain that thousands more were forthcoming. Nor did she have any desire to stay in the country—much less, the house—where her husband had come to such a tragic end.

She and her children found compassion in an unlikely place. They were taken in by a Turkish couple who lived not far from them. Though Muslims, they were appalled at the unprovoked brutality of their countrymen. They were ashamed and apologetic. They had watched and admired the Momjian family for years. Now they would house Emma and her four children. If necessary, they would hide them.

It was several days after the murderous rampage before Emma dared to venture out again into Antakya. The village she loved looked like a war zone. Armenian homes bore the scars of the violence: windows were broken and doors splintered. Some homes had been burned to the ground. Far worse, families were broken. Wives were now widows. Children were now orphans. And she knew that things would get worse, not better. When mobs stopped killing, disease and starvation started. Already, the stench of the town was revolting.

Emma's children were traumatized. James, her oldest, was sick, and now injured. And the violence could recommence at any time. She felt as though death were stalking them, merely awaiting the whim of the mad sultan or the reignited passions of a merciless mob. Traveling was dangerous, but not so dangerous as staying. But where could her young family go, and how would they travel? She had no husband to protect her and no father to care for her children. The Momjians had nowhere to turn for help.

Providentially, help came to them.

Horrific times breed heroic deeds. A bright spot in the travesty of the Armenian Genocide is the courage and compassion shown to Armenian refugees by Protestant German missionaries, whose gospel labors in one of the most difficult places in the world is a convicting example to us today.[63] The orphanages run by German Lutherans met a desperate need.

There is certainly irony in the fact that help for Armenian orphans came from Germans. It was the nation of Germany, led by its powerful and omni-ambitious Kaiser Wilhelm II, which manipulated the nation of Turkey into becoming its ally in World War I—or more accurately, its puppet. Turkey was on the brink of collapse. The once great Ottoman Empire had already lost over half of its territory, carved up and divided among the more modern and stable nations that surrounded Turkey on every side. Turkey was bankrupt, pleading for loans from

---

[63] The missionaries' almost reckless compassion reminds me of Phil Golson, a friend with a doctorate in music who left his career in education to take the gospel to the corrupt and needy country of South Africa. "Mission work is not safe," he says. "It's not supposed to be safe. But it's necessary, and it's right." Praise God for such courage—now in South Africa and a century ago amid the terrors of Turkey.

European nations and the United States. They desperately needed help catching up with the rest of the modern world—help with their infrastructure, their economy, and their military. Great Britain had been a help for a time but had recently poached Egypt from the Ottoman Empire. America was opting for neutrality, and most of its help came in the form of missionaries and educators. Germany was the obvious source of assistance to the Turkish regime—but German help came with a price. By the beginning of World War I, Germany had shrewdly and effectively commandeered the Turkish military, gaining millions of soldiers, control of the Bosphorus Strait, and a naval presence in the Mediterranean.

Their alliance with Germany emboldened the Turks, and they felt more secure defying the rest of the West in their persecution of the Armenians. The Turks used the Great War as a cover to recommence Abdul Hamid's plan to exterminate the Armenians still among them. Slaughtering one million of their most productive citizens—during a time when the entire nation should have been mobilized for the war effort—was psychopathic. The German government had almost complete sway over the Turks, and they could certainly have intervened. Instead, the German leadership chose complicit silence.

And yet, German missionaries were among those who most frequently helped Armenians in the wake of the slaughter, as if determined to compensate for their ruthless rulers. Ambassador Morgenthau said as much, based on his repeated correspondence with German missionaries: "They did not conceal the humiliation that they felt, as Germans, in the fact that their own nation was allied with a people that could perpetrate such infamies."[64]

———————

It had been almost a month since the murderous rampage that claimed Sarkis Momjian's life and left his family defenseless. Multi-

———————

[64] Morgenthau, *Ambassador Morgenthau's Story*, 220.

tudes of people from Antakya and surrounding towns languished. Few had been shown the kindness which Emma and her children received from their neighbors, with whom they continued to live in exchange for performing basic domestic duties. Many of their Armenian neighbors were homeless. More were sick. All were hungry.

As hope waned, a convoy of trucks and wagons pulled into town, bringing desperately needed aid. The Armenians, who had prayed for a miracle, greeted the evangelical German missionaries as though they had been sent from heaven. In a way, they had. In obedience to Christ's Great Commission, they had gone to the world's most dangerous country to help the world's most needy people. They had come to Turkey to evangelize Muslims, but most of their fruit had come from the Armenians who already knew of Christ but needed to be taught about grace.[65] The Germans brought the gospel, but they also brought material help. As news of their arrival passed through Antakya, crowds of grateful Armenians went to meet them, cheering and even weeping as they escorted them into town.

Although the crowds were overwhelming, Emma was stunned at the efficiency of the missionaries. The morning after their arrival, everyone in need of food had been warmed by a hearty broth. In the afternoon, the entire town enjoyed a simple but life-giving stew. Doctors and nurses tended the wounded and the sick as best as they could in such primitive and desperate circumstances.

In addition to receiving nourishment, the Armenians—refugees in their own village—were given a purpose. They were organized and enlisted as part of the relief process. Some helped cook the immense amount of food. Some were set to work providing medical care. Farmers were supplied with money for seed and tools so the relief would continue long after the foreigners departed.

---

[65] Franz Werfel writes in his historical novel *The Forty Days of Musa Dagh*, "Syria and Anatolia contained a great many Protestants and . . . the Evangelical church had those German and American missionaries who had cared so well for Armenian orphans and victims to thank for those converts." Franz Werfel, *The Forty Days of Musa Dagh*, trans. Geoffrey Dunlop and James Reidel (Boston, MA: Verba Mundi Books, 2012), 79.

The Germans' stay in Antakya was only a few weeks in duration. The missionaries had met immediate needs and prepared the Armenians to meet their own needs. Knowing that another cycle of terror was inevitable, they urged the crowds to seek shelter outside Turkey. They themselves were returning to their base in Beirut, Lebanon, only two hundred miles to the south, but a harbor from the horrors of eastern Turkey.

Generously, and tragically, the German believers offered to take children with them and care for them in Beirut orphanages. They gave Emma the chance to send her three youngest children to safety. Imagine her dilemma at hearing the offer. A few months before, the thought of entrusting her children to strangers would have seemed like a crime. Now, everything in the world had turned upside down. *Keeping* her own children felt reckless.

Every fiber of Emma's being wanted to keep her young children, just eight, six, and four years old. They had already experienced enough trauma to last a lifetime. But she knew that the best protection and provision they could receive would have to come elsewhere, from others. No realization is more devastating for a mother—or more selfless—than knowing that she cannot adequately care for her own children. Emma knew.

———

Emma planned to seek passage to America, where she had an uncle who would take her in. Taking her entire family was impossible. Faced with an excruciating decision, she determined to go ahead with James to America and then send for the three other children when she could. Her family was being dismembered.

"Imagine that," Panosian challenged, as he related the story. "She left her children, an ocean away. The oldest, my mother, was eight. Think of your own children." His voice filled with emotion and wonder, then fell silent.

Panosian doesn't know what the heart-rending goodbyes looked like. Certainly there were tears. Perhaps there was an attempt at fortitude. Undoubtedly there were expressions of love, perhaps punctuated by the kind of rapid-fire orders every mother in every culture gives to her children: "Take care of each other. Obey these kind people. Make your father and me proud." Very likely, there were terrible groans which cannot be uttered, but which are not unheard.[66]

Leaving her children in the care of strangers was the most difficult part of the entire hellish experience, more painful even than the murder of her husband. Emma would continue, somehow, for their sake. But she must have envied Sarkis for being spared that dreadful day.

---

[66] Romans 8:26.

CHAPTER ELEVEN

BROTHERS

"A brother is born for adversity."

—Proverbs 17:17

The Panosian family had grown since Nazar's departure to become a cobbler's apprentice. His stepmother had given birth to a little girl. Of course, the new child—the couple's own—was the favorite. Worse, the girl seemed to know it. Even at just three years of age, it was clear to her that her stepbrother Manuel must bow to her wishes. Such lessons can endure for a lifetime, especially for the one accustomed to taking.

Manny's life was small and bland. He struggled to remember his mother, whose face had grown dim in his memory. She, like Nazar, had left him behind. Though his memories were scant, he knew that she was kind, especially compared to his stepmother. He at least remembered that he missed her. He also missed his brother. He recalled the fateful day when Nazar left their home and began his apprenticeship. He clung to Nazar's promise to return for him, though that hope was fading like his recollection of their mother.

Finally, seven years after making the promise, Nazar Panosian kept his word. He returned to Balan, and to his brother, a remarkably different person from the one who had left. He was a strapping boy of seventeen. A man, really, for adolescence didn't exist in the Turkey of the early nineteenth century.

His return resuscitated the failing spirits of his little brother. Nazar wasted no time in sharing his ambitions with Manny. He had mastered shoemaking, thanks to the Turkish cobbler. His apprenticeship was finished, and he was ready to launch out on his own. He had dreamed of owning his own business for years, and finally the time had come. All he needed now was an apprentice of his own—a partner!

Manny didn't need to be asked twice. He left his home and never looked back. Nazar's passion and confidence were contagious. They found a space in Balan for their startup business. They acquired supplies. Nazar began making shoes, taking every opportunity to share his exceptional skills with Manny. Ever so slowly, they began making money.

Nazar's ambitions were nothing short of audacious. He dreamed big, and he worked tirelessly to make his hopes a reality. Six months into their partnership, seeing his brother's progress, he finally unveiled his ultimate intentions. He knew that the future was in the West, not in Turkey. He was weary of the unlevel playing field—the Turks' unjust taxation of the Armenians, their threats, and their outright thievery. After working for a Turk, and experiencing none of these unjust impediments to success, it was difficult to return to the "normalcy" of persecution. He longed for security and unbridled opportunity, and he knew these were unattainable for an Armenian in Turkey.

He told Manny of an uncle—their mother's brother—who lived in America. He shared his plan to immigrate to the United States, where he and Manny could forge a new life together.

Manny would probably never have considered such a massive move on his own. But he believed Nazar could do anything! He wasn't just his big brother. He was his mentor and his hero. If Nazar believed they needed to make the move, it was settled. He would do everything in his power to repay his brother's kindness.

They showed uncommon resolve. They were industrious in their work and relentlessly frugal in their spending. They needed enough money for passage to America, and they each needed twenty-five American dollars once they reached Ellis Island, the entryway to their Promised Land. They worked, and saved, and dreamed.

In 1913, almost a year into their grand endeavor, the brothers were less than halfway to their goal, despite their diligence. They could work no harder, but their wages were paltry, and taxes were painfully high. Both brothers feared that their dream might never become a reality. They watched the political landscape warily. Though there hadn't been a repetition of the slaughters of 1894–1896, the future of Armenians was still precarious, despite the promises of the newly formed government, "the Young Turks."

Together, the two young men reached a difficult but necessary decision. If they waited until they could go to America together, they might never make it. If one went ahead, he could earn much more, then send for the other. It was either one at a time or none at all. Nazar, the older and more gifted of the two brothers, would go to America first. It was settled.

A few months later, the boys made the trip to Alexandretta (modern Iskenderun), the port town on the eastern edge of the Mediterranean. From there, Nazar would sail across the Mediterranean, through the Strait of Gibraltar, and then across the Atlantic to the "Canaan" of America.

Both brothers were struck by the ironic repetition of events. Once again, Nazar was venturing out and Manny was staying behind. Once again, the older brother made a promise to the younger. Nazar would make a start, and then he would bring Manny to America.

Both prayed the promise could be kept.

CHAPTER TWELVE

"GIVE ME YOUR TIRED . . ."

1910 — ANTAKYA, TURKEY
AND ELLIS ISLAND, NEW YORK

*"Immigrants aboard their transatlantic steamships
often responded with tears or shouts of joy when they
first spotted the Statue of Liberty, but as their steamers
chugged past the bronze marvel, a more foreboding sight
came into view. . . . Italian immigrants often referred to
Ellis Island as* l'Isola dell Lagrime, *the 'Island of Tears.'"*

—Tyler Anbinder[67]

Armenians were frugal people. Though taxed beyond reason, they still managed to prosper. In many ways, they were the backbone of Turkey's economy. They displayed such industry and thrift that they often managed to accumulate significantly more wealth than their Muslim neighbors. Their financial success gave rise to charges that their riches came at Turkey's expense, which was preposterous. The opposite was true: when Turkey annihilated the Armenians, it eliminated its most productive citizens and committed economic suicide.

Armenians invested their savings in a unique fashion, as Panosian explains:

> They didn't use banks. They didn't believe in banks. They didn't *trust* banks. Whatever excess wealth a family had would be turned into gold in the form of jewels: chains, bracelets, and so forth. It was not ostentation. It was savings!

---

[67] Tyler Anbinder, *City of Dreams: The 400-Year Epic History of Immigrant New York* (Boston, MA: Houghton Mifflin Harcourt, 2016), 329.

The Armenians had lived on the precipice of disaster for centuries. They knew that a hasty flight to safety was a likely part of their future. Gold chains were small, portable, and universally valuable.

Emma Momjian had managed to protect her family's cache of jewelry during the violence. Her husband's murderers had taken food, but they had missed what was most valuable. She knew she must make her escape before the dreaded Ottomans returned to take her savings, or her life. It was time to sell, then flee.

As expected, scores of Armenian women were selling their jewelry. It was a virtual "run on the bank," the bank being Turkish jewelers or street corner hucksters. Also as expected, the supply drove the prices down. Shrewdly, Emma asked her Muslim neighbor to conduct her business on her behalf, certain that he would be given a better price than a helpless Armenian widow. He willingly did so, exchanging her beautiful jewelry for enough cash to get her and her sickly son out of Antakya, and even out of Turkey.

Emma secured passage for two on a ship headed for America. She and James took their leave of their kind Muslim neighbors. Once again, the neighbor couple voiced their deep grief and humiliation over how the Momjian family and other Armenians had been treated. Emma would never forget their kindness.

Emma set her sights now on America. She had an uncle in Binghamton, New York. Dick Davidian, her mother's brother, had arrived in America years earlier. Armenian immigrants would cluster in various locations, preserving their language and culture even as they assimilated into the rest of American life. Binghamton was home to a large number of Armenian immigrants.

Emma and James boarded the ship out of Alexandretta. They took little with them, and they were glad. The dock was chaotic as people said hasty goodbyes and clambered aboard, fearful that the corrupt Turkish police would jerk them out of line just as they were about to make their escape. Some officials were glad to be rid of them; some rued the thought of any Christians surviving, much less having the hope of a bright future in America. Thankfully, providentially, they were allowed to board the ship.

Conditions on board were starkly different. Pensive quiet replaced the chaos. Many of the Momjians' fellow passengers were Christians of seemingly every nationality, unspeakably relieved to be escaping from Turkey with their lives, but also deeply saddened by what they had experienced. There was a death-like silence. Words were incapable of conveying what was in their hearts, so they said nothing. Many, like Emma, were leaving family members behind, some living, some dead. There was no joy—just relief mingled with guilt.

When the ship finally sailed several hours later, the Momjians watched their homeland fade from view. Neither Emma nor James would ever return to Turkey. Nor would they desire to.

The baby in Emma's womb would not survive. The Panosians don't know what happened to the child—only that Emma was forced to bear yet another sorrow. Dr. Panosian comments, "The baby just did not survive. It is known to God."

Within a few months, Emma had lost her husband and her unborn child. She was now putting an ocean between herself and three of her children. She had entrusted them to godly missionaries who had left their own families and risked their own lives to care for them. More importantly, she had entrusted them to the God who has revealed Himself to be the Father of the fatherless.[68]

There are an estimated half million Armenians in the United States today. At the beginning of the twentieth century, there were fewer than ten thousand.[69] Emma and James Momjian were ahead of the curve. Like most immigrants who crossed the Atlantic to reach America, they would ultimately disembark on New York City's Ellis Island. Before landing on Ellis Island, they were greeted by Bedloe Island's[70] Statue of Liberty, the enormous hostess of their new homeland:

---

[68] Psalm 68:5.
[69] Peter Balakian, *The Burning Tigris*, 20.
[70] Bedloe Island was renamed Liberty Island in 1956.

Give me your tired, your poor,
Your huddled masses yearning to breathe free,
The wretched refuse of your teeming shore.
Send these, the homeless, tempest-tossed to me,
I lift my lamp beside the golden door![71]

To Americans, Ellis Island represents hope, freedom, and welcome. But to the immigrants who first arrived there—over twelve million from its opening on January 1, 1892, to its closure on November 12, 1954—it was far from inviting. After risking everything to come to America, and after enduring grueling journeys across the Atlantic in cramped and squalid ships, immigrants now had to fret about whether they would actually be let in. It wasn't a given. Ellis Island was a place of inspection, interrogation, and sometimes quarantine. For some, it was a place of rejection. Imagine arriving so close to the American "Paradise," only to be sent back to the very country you had fled. For some, Lady Liberty was a sentry, not a hostess.

Debates over immigration policies are nothing new. If anything, the debate over granting asylum to refugees was more volatile a century ago than it is today. Chinese immigrants were rejected altogether. Even Europeans were looked upon as a threat to American society. As one historian of American immigration writes, "There were fears that America was becoming a dumping ground for Europe's unwanted peasants."[72] So much for Lady Liberty's invitation to "the wretched refuse." Much of the rhetoric about immigration at the turn of the twentieth century, even from statesmen, was unabashedly racist. Foreigners who aspired to become immigrants had to demonstrate their worth.

"The great judgment" began on board the ships. Before the passengers were even allowed to disembark, a physician would come aboard and inspect each individual, especially looking for signs of infectious diseases like cholera and typhus. This took hours—sometimes days.

---

[71] Emma Lazarus' sonnet "The New Colossus" hangs on a plaque inside the pedestal of the Statue of Liberty.

[72] Vincent J. Cannato, *American Passage: The History of Ellis Island* (New York: Harper Perennial, 2010), 40.

Eventually, each passenger would be tagged by dockworkers, would gather up his possessions, and would proceed onto the island itself.

Having waited on the ship, the would-be immigrants now waited in the iconic brick and limestone building that is the inspection station. It was built to be sturdy, replacing the wooden structure that burned down in 1897. It was not built to be comfortable or quiet. It was a stiflingly hot, painfully loud place that inevitably wreaked of body odor. Every day, thousands of people waited on tile floors and trudged between endless iron railings, seeking the correct stalls where the interpreters who spoke their languages would walk them through yet another inspection.

Immigration officers were specially trained to look for those who were deemed unfit for the United States. Some looked for signs of poor health—a limp, a cough, an unhealthy look in the eye, even flat feet. Throughout the process, those who were suspected of some disqualifying condition were tagged with chalk on their shoulder, signaling that they needed to be examined more closely. Men were separated from women and inspected for venereal diseases. Women were stripped to the waist and inspected by physicians—a harrowing and humiliating experience for them.

Besides the physical exams, inspectors looked for evidence of reasonable intelligence. Immigration officials tried to avoid admitting those who might be a burden on American society. The Immigration Act of 1907 forbade entrance to those who were deemed unworthy:

> All idiots, imbeciles, feebleminded persons, epileptics, insane persons, and persons who have been insane within five years previous; persons who have had two or more attacks of insanity at any time previously; paupers; persons likely to become a public charge; professional beggars; persons afflicted with tuberculosis or with a loathsome or dangerous contagious disease; persons not comprehended within any of the foregoing excluded classes who are found to be and are certified by the examining surgeon as being mentally or physically defective, such mental or physical defect being of a nature which may affect the ability of such alien to earn a living.[73]

---

[73] U.S. Immigration Act of 1907. Available at https://www.loc.gov/law/help/statutes-at-large/59th-congress/session-2/c59s2ch1134.pdf. Accessed August 8, 2018.

In short, in the words of Vincent J. Cannato, "If immigrants were to be allowed into the country, they needed to prove they were healthy and self-sufficient."[74]

Immigration officials detained unaccompanied women, who all too often were forced into a life of prostitution. Women could leave the island only if accompanied or met by a responsible male. As misogynistic as that may sound, it was intended to protect the immigrants even as it protected society. Naïve immigrants were easy prey to "runners," hoodlums who stole their belongings, sold them bogus railway tickets, and enslaved them into lives of poverty and prostitution.

Beyond requirements related to health and intelligence, immigrants needed to give an address where they would be living, and they needed to possess $25 to get started (roughly $650 in our day), often in addition to the fare required to get to their destination. The $25 "economic test" wasn't law; it had been considered and rejected by Congress. But it was still the *de facto* law, thanks to the zealous (some would say inhumane) policies of William Williams, the head of immigration on Ellis Island from 1902 to 1905 and from 1909 to 1914. Williams was dubbed "the Haman of Ellis Island."[75] A law unto himself, Williams tightened all immigration standards in an attempt to correct the kinder, gentler approach to immigrants that characterized the three years of his absence from Ellis Island, 1906–1908. Tyler Anbinder explains in his history of immigrant New York, *City of Dreams:*

> When Williams took charge again at the end of May 1909 [just a year before Emma Momjian's immigration], he immediately announced that the more welcoming attitude toward immigrants that had previously characterized the administration of Ellis Island would not continue. "We are receiving too many low-grade immigrants," Williams told the press. He vowed to enforce the existing immigration laws far more strictly than his predecessor and weed

---

[74] Cannato, *American Passage,* 8.
[75] Haman was the enemy of the Jews in the Old Testament book of Esther—a notorious man with murderous intent.

out the "unintelligent," immigrants "of low vitality," and those whose lack of savings indicated that they did not possess the intellect or work ethic necessary to succeed in the United States.[76]

Louis Adamic, who immigrated to the United States in 1913, recalls his final inspection, which took place in the massive Registry Room (known as the Great Hall):

> The examiner sat bureaucratically—very much in the manner of officials in the Old Country—behind a great desk, which stood upon a high platform. On the wall above him was a picture of George Washington. Beneath it was an American flag. The official spoke a bewildering mixture of many Slavic languages. He had a stern voice and a sour visage. I had difficulty understanding some of his questions. At a small table, piled with papers, not far from the examiner's desk, was a clerk who called out our names, which, it seemed, were written on the long sheets of paper before him. When my turn came, toward dusk, I was asked the usual questions. When and where was I born? My nationality? Religion? Was I a legitimate child? What were the names of my parents? Was I an imbecile? Was I a prostitute? . . . Was I an ex-convict? A criminal? Why had I come to the United States? I was questioned as to the state of my finances, and I produced the required twenty-five dollars. What did I expect to do in the United States? I replied that I hoped to get a job. What kind of a job? I didn't know; any kind of job.[77]

After a lifetime of planning, weeks of travel, and hours of waiting in line, the fate of each immigrant ultimately came down to a single interview which usually lasted around sixty seconds.

Desperate as they were, Emma Momjian and her son James survived the rigors of Ellis Island. They were allowed access to the United States despite James' physical frailty, probably because they were refugees from a dangerous land. They waited. They endured the inspections. They answered the questions. They were held in a detention area, awaiting their male escort. Eventually, they were met by Emma's Uncle Dick and taken 185 miles northwest to his home in Binghamton, New

[76] Anbinder, *City of Dreams*, 343.
[77] Louis Adamic, *Laughing in the Jungle: The Autobiography of an American Immigrant* (New York: Harper and Brothers, 1932), 41–45.

York. They knew no one else. They spoke no English. But finally, they were safe.

Were Emma's other children safe? She didn't know, and she wouldn't for another nine years.

CHAPTER THIRTEEN

"FRÖHLICHE WEIHNACHTEN"

1911 — BEIRUT, LEBANON

*"Unless the open hands of charity be reached out . . . hunger
and cold will gather victims by the tens of thousands and
bury them like the falling leaves beneath the snow."*

—Clara Barton, founder of the American Red Cross[78]

Books detailing the horrors of the genocide are filled with ghastly
pictures of malnourished children who appear to be more skeleton
than flesh. "Think of the starving Armenians!" The American ad cam-
paign was an appropriate charge, for there were indeed Armenians
who were starving. But in God's providence—and thanks to heroic
missionaries and a heartbroken mother who knew her limitations—
the Momjian children would not be among them.

Sara, Rose, and Mihran rocked back and forth in the back of a
large military-type transport truck. They were surrounded by other
children, all of whom were jostled and bounced by every bump in the
uneven road. Some of them the Momjian children recognized from
their hometown of Antakya. Most were strangers to them. But all had
the same vacant look in their eyes, as though they were unable to process the horrors they had witnessed. In the last few months, their lives
had been torn to shreds. Their homes, their possessions, and their par-

---

[78] Clara Barton, appealing to Americans to give to help "the starving Armenians" in 1896.
Americans did so, championing the cause of the Armenians in a way that launched the unprecedented American humanitarian efforts of the twentieth century. Quoted in Merle Curti, *American Philanthropy Abroad* (New Brunswick, NJ: Rutgers University Press, 1963), 124–125.

ents were gone. Some huddled with brothers and sisters. Many were utterly alone.

The caravan of trucks and traumatized children snaked its way south. Their intended destination was Beirut, Lebanon, just over two hundred miles from Antakya, on the eastern edge of the Mediterranean. Beirut was a safe harbor. That's a jarring sentence to those of us familiar with the brutal civil wars that consumed the city during the late twentieth century. However, at the commencement of the twentieth century, Lebanon was a virtual "demilitarized zone." Because of its strategic location, Beirut was a cosmopolitan city—a cultural, ethnic, and religious melting pot in an otherwise Islamic area. It was an important economic capital in the region, as valuable to European investors as to Turkey. Because of its financial significance, it was immune to the violence that raged all around it. And because of its immunity, it became the mecca of missions and humanitarian aid.

The German evangelicals prayed that they would be able to complete the journey to Beirut without being ambushed by the Turks all around them. Many Muslims wanted the Armenians terminated, not exiled. But few would dare to cross western missionaries—especially Germans, whose leaders were wooing Turkey into an alliance in the years leading up to the Great War. Still, sanity had already been sacrificed to hatred. The missionaries were unsure when the Turks' wrath might pour out upon them, and they were eager to get their human cargo out of harm's way.

The mournful caravan arrived at the mission in Beirut after three days of wearying travel. The children were greeted by kind, efficient missionaries—more evangelicals from Germany. They were welcomed by the head of the mission, whom Sara would recall throughout the rest of her life as "the Deaconess."

It was immediately evident that they were in a safe place, among good people. The mission was remarkably clean. The children there were noticeably happy and well cared for. They were assured that they would be given shelter—and instructed that they must all do their part and "pitch in" as long as they were at the mission.

All of this was settling to the children, including the Momjians. But there was one piece of news that must have shattered their new-found peace: the boys and girls would live in separate locations. The policy makes perfect sense, even a century later, but it must have been excruciating to the children to endure yet another separation. Four-year-old Mihran was taken from his older sisters, who probably felt the sting more keenly and enduringly than he did.

Several weeks had passed since their arrival at the orphanage. The girls had been able to see Mihran regularly. He was more than fine, enjoying his scores of new "brothers." Both Sara and Rose were a help at the orphanage—a credit to the training they had received from their mother. Their skills expanded under the instruction of the Deaconess, as Dr. Panosian explains:

> They were taught German. They had daily Bible reading and prayers. They were taught a catechism. They learned domestic arts, like cooking, sewing, and cleaning. Mother [Sara] learned everything a young lady needs to know, in terms of running a household.

The transition was more difficult for Sara than for her younger siblings. Deeper memories make change harder. She mourned their many losses, and she would cry quietly each night. Her grief consumed her appetite. In response to her reluctance to eat, the Deaconess would regularly give Sara cod liver oil. It was miserable—and motivating. When Sara mentioned to the other girls how much she detested it, they told her she wouldn't have to take it if she would only eat normal meals like everyone else. She did, and the cod liver oil treatments ceased, much to her relief.

The orphanage was run by many deaconesses—essentially the Protestant counterpart to Catholic nuns. They had devoted their lives to God and to these children, the neediest children in the world at the time. They were godly women. The best of them all, though, was Sara's Deaconess. She had taken Sara under her wing from their first meeting. She saw the girl's deep grief, but she also saw her potential and admired her dependability. She relied on her almost as much as she did on the other missionaries, both because there was so much to be done and because she knew Sara needed the distraction. The Deaconess made a deep, lifelong impression on Sara.

A significant longing for Sara, which only increased her sorrow, was the approach of the first Christmas since her family's tragedies. All her young life she had anticipated Christmas with her family. As the close of the year neared, she wondered if Germans even celebrated Christmas. No one mentioned it, and she didn't dare ask. She was fortunate to be alive, she knew—fortunate to be safe, and clothed, and fed. She tried to be grateful. She *was* grateful. But she felt an emptiness. Panosian shares the story as it was passed down to him:

> My mother told about the anticipation of Christmas. She saw no preparation of any kind at the orphanage for the coming of Christmas. Until Christmas Eve! And then they rolled back room dividers, and suddenly they revealed a Christmas tree, with lights, and ornaments, and a single gift for every one of the children.

"Fröhliche Weihnachten," shouted the German missionaries. "Merry Christmas!" The children were entirely surprised, and they were as happy as they had ever been. Normally, the orphanage offered adequate but simple food. But at Christmas, they indulged. Each of the children enjoyed Christmas cookies, special foods, and a simple gift. Sara treasured hers as though it were a handful of diamonds. Panosian again picks up the story:

> Mother's gift was a little pin cushion—a sewing cushion—which looked like an apple, made of felt, stiffened. And it had a removable top, and in the top were pins and so forth. She kept that to her dying day. [Here his voice softened with emotion, and cracked slightly.] She had that evidence of Christmas at the orphanage until she died at the age of eighty-five, years later. It was such a revelation. "There is Christmas here, after all."

This was a turning point for Sara. It healed some deep wounds. Her father had been murdered. Her mother and brother were far away, if they were even alive. Her entire life had been splintered. But there was still someone who loved them: the godly Deaconess who read them Scripture every night, and the other Christian ladies who cared for them. There was still Christmas—even with Germans, even in Beirut. And there was still Christ. All of these thoughts she treasured up in her heart to be remembered for a lifetime. Like pins in a pin cushion.

CHAPTER FOURTEEN

THE LAND OF OPPORTUNITY

1913 — ELLIS ISLAND, NEW YORK
DETROIT, MICHIGAN
AND BINGHAMTON, NEW YORK

*"No one story encapsulates the Ellis Island experiences; there
are literally millions. For most immigrants, Ellis Island was
a gateway to a new life in America. It was an integral part of
their American passage. It would become a special place for some
immigrants and their families, while others retained only faint
memories of the place or saw it as a site of unimaginable emotional
stress filled with stern government officials who possessed the power
to decide their fate. For a small percentage of people, Ellis Island
was all they would see of America before being sent back home."*

—Vincent J. Cannato[79]

Before Ellis Island became the gateway to America, it was a gateway to eternity, at least for a time. In the late eighteenth and early nineteenth centuries it was called "Gibbet Island." The name had a gory significance. On Gibbet Island, the United States government hanged condemned pirates on a gibbet, or gallows, and left them on public display as a deterrent to piracy.

Fast forward several decades. After Ellis Island was used as the gateway to America, it was a prison where "enemy aliens" were kept during World War II. Secluding prisoners on an island isn't a new concept. Think of Alcatraz, off the coast of San Francisco. Or the beauti-

---

[79] Cannato, *American Passage*, 5.

ful Chateau d'If in France, made famous by Alexander Dumas' novel *The Count of Monte Cristo.* Or Robben Island, where Nelson Mandela was held just off the coast of Capetown in South Africa. Or Elba, which held the defeated Napoleon for almost a year, or even Patmos, where the apostle John was imprisoned. Ellis Island was utilized as a prison for a time for the same reason—the water around the island was as effective as walls and fences are at keeping the prisoners away from the public. Ellis Island contained those deemed dangerous, much like the other islands in New York City which housed the insane, the orphaned, or the quarantined.[80]

The comparison is significant. Before it was a prison, Ellis Island held weary and worried immigrants for the same reason: to protect the citizens of the United States from those who were considered "undesirables" for reasons of poor health, weak minds, or empty pockets. Ellis Island was a gate, but it was locked until those who wanted to gain entrance were carefully vetted to prove their worth.

One might wonder, then, if immigrants posed such a great threat, why admit them to the United States at all? In part, because it was the American way; almost *all* Americans are immigrants. In part, because America was truly benevolent, welcoming those seeking asylum from difficult parts of the world. But there was also a less altruistic motive. America was expanding. Industrialization was booming. And that meant there was an enormous need for workers. Enter the European immigrant—or twelve million European immigrants, to be precise. Immigrants, especially in the early decades of the 1900s, were "a source of cheap labor to power the new industrial economy."[81]

That may sound opportunistic or manipulative to modern ears. To Nazar Panosian, it sounded like paradise! He wanted a chance to work hard, to prove himself, and perhaps to prosper. To be part of a great workforce was the very reason he had left his brother Manuel in Turkey. He wanted to start a new life, then bring his brother to share

[80] Cannato, *American Passage,* 24.
[81] Cannato, *American Passage,* 13.

it. Their dream was the dream of every immigrant and of every family member who had stayed behind in hopes of reuniting in the Promised Land of America.

This is an important point to understand. Nazar Panosian's immigration to the United States wasn't so much a flight from oppression as a pursuit of opportunity. Turkey was hostile to Armenians, as always, but the threat in 1913 wasn't any worse than it had been for the last eighteen years, since the massacres of 1895. He came primarily as an entrepreneur, not as a refugee. And he had every reason to expect not only his own success, but his reunion with Manny in the near future. Armenians were accustomed to hardship, but no one suspected impending tragedy. Genocide survivor Grigoris Balakian describes the mindset of most Armenians in the Ottoman Empire at the time: "No one considered leaving the country because, unfortunately, no one anticipated any immediate danger."[82]

Nazar had sailed from Alexandretta, Turkey, crossing the Mediterranean, passing through the Strait of Gibraltar between Spain and Morocco, and finally crossing the mighty Atlantic. Like most immigrants, he traveled as a "steerage passenger" in cramped quarters below deck. It was miserable for the passengers but highly lucrative for the companies running the steamships.

After the transatlantic journey of two to three weeks, Nazar's ship finally pulled into New York Harbor. He had brought little—his clothing, some tools, and the $25 which would be required of him when he reached Ellis Island. Only the basics and his boundless ambitions. Nazar cheered with the rest of the ship's passengers when they first spotted Lady Liberty on nearby Bedloe Island. But they grew ominously quiet as the ship slowly docked on Ellis Island.

Every would-be immigrant had heard of the looming inspections, and many of them rehearsed their answers, fearful of making the greatest mistake of their lives.

---

[82] Grigoris Balakian, *Armenian Golgotha*, 49.

Nazar faced no real peril. At nineteen, he was young and fit. He was a skilled worker. And he had the $25 required to gain entrance to the United States. Though the money wasn't collected by the inspectors, it had to be displayed as proof that the immigrant wouldn't immediately become an indigent once in the United States.

Despite his enthusiasm, there was no rushing this process. Like the millions of other immigrants who came before and after him, it was time for him to wait. He easily managed his few belongings. He felt for the people who were struggling with their children, or perhaps their aged parents, along with all their worldly possessions. When possible, he helped someone carry a trunk. He heard a dizzying number of dialects all around him. But the faces all bore the stress of those whose fates were anything but secure. Occasionally, Nazar would see the agony a family experienced when an immigrant got a second look from an inspector, or worse, had a chalk mark scribbled on his sleeve to indicate a possible physical or mental defect. Though he often didn't understand the nervous chatter caused by the dreaded mark, he could guess what the fearful families said. How terrible it would be to come so far—to be so close—and to be turned away!

Fortunately, Nazar attracted no such attention. He was clearly healthy and intelligent. The inspectors barely bothered to look at him, several just jerking their heads to tell him to move along. Young men like Nazar could feel almost ignored throughout the whole process.

When he was through with the physical examinations, Nazar encountered the din of the Registry Room, the cavernous and raucous hall where immigrants faced the final questions that would determine their future. He waited and watched, feeling like a racehorse held back by the starting gate. He wanted to get off this island and get started with his new life! Still, there were rows of lines to walk through, kept separate by a maze of iron railings.

Finally, Nazar neared the final inspector. He heard others being asked questions in his native Armenian tongue. "From where have you come? Where are you going? How will you make your living? Do you intend to learn English? Do you have any infectious diseases? Are you an imbecile? Were you ever in prison? Do you have $25 to support yourself until you find work?"

Nazar's nimble mind was mentally answering the questions before they were even finished: "Turkey. Detroit. Cobbler. Yes. No. No. No. Yes. This is easy! Hurry!"

At last, there was but one person in front of him. Like everyone else, the man was nervous. He was dressed in his very best, hoping to make a good impression. But his shirt was drenched with sweat, like everyone else's, and it stuck to his body. Despite the man's obvious anxiety, Nazar had observed enough during the endless wait to know that *this* man had nothing to worry about. He was exactly the kind of person who would thrive in America. Surely he would get through with no problem.

The inspector, as hot and irritable as everyone else, concluded the interview by asking to see the man's $25. The man hesitated, then explained that he had had some unexpected expenses during his passage. He had most of it, and he could certainly get more when he met his American family. He was just a little short. The inspector folded his arms and raised his voice: "The rule is the same for everybody. You want to get through, show me your $25." He raised his eyes and lectured the crowd. "Have your papers ready, and *make sure* you have your $25!" The Armenian man blanched. Surely he hadn't come this far only to be sent away over a few dollars. Tears filled his eyes, and he made a show of looking in his pockets and bags. Nazar knew people, and he could tell there was no more money to be found.

Nazar whispered to his countryman, "How much do you need?" The man explained that he was just a few dollars short. Nazar instinctively made up the difference, handing the man several dollars. The man embraced him like a brother, overwhelmed with gratitude. Handing the inspector the required total, he gathered his belongings and proceeded to begin his American dream. Nazar smiled. It felt good to have helped someone in need.

After hours of sweltering heat and unending lines, Nazar's time had finally come. He answered the questions with confidence. "I come from Turkey. . . . I am a cobbler. . . . I am going to join my uncle in Detroit. . . ."

It took only moments. Everything was in order. But then he was asked to produce his $25. Suddenly a pain of panic shot through his chest. Dr. Panosian shares the story he heard countless times from his father Nazar:

> He realized that he himself was short. He came to Ellis Island with $25. And he gave some of it away. It was an impulse rather than a thought-through action. To me, it was a reflection of his char-acter—that without thinking of the consequences, it just seemed like the right thing to do for a fellow human being, for a fellow Armenian.

For the first time, Nazar doubted his own admittance into the United States. For the first time, he felt the angst of those who had received a chalk mark on their shoulder to indicate some deficiency. He was helpless.

Dr. Panosian again picks up the story, his voice welling up with emotion: "The observant inspector, who had seen the whole transac-tion, shared enough human kindness to let Dad through."

For all the legends about the officials at Ellis Island bullying immigrants or changing their names, most of it is untrue. Testimony exists to prove that many agents were humane, and that they gener-ally didn't look to make the already uneasy immigrants suffer. Tyler Anbinder describes situations almost identical to Nazar's in *City of Dreams,* his history of New York City:

> The immigration inspectors in the Registry Room who guarded what H. G. Wells aptly called 'the gate of America' had enormous control over the fate of each immigrant. Decades later, newcomers recalled with gratitude the officer who had waved them past even though they had only $22 instead of the required $25, or who did not ask to see their money at all, or who had suggested that an immigrant rethink his answer when, out of nervousness or igno-rance, he gave a reply that might get him turned away.[83]

---

[83] Anbinder, *City of Dreams,* 350–351.

Nazar Panosian was waved through. He had received back some of
the kindness he had shown. His dreams were coming true. He wasn't
yet an American citizen. But he was an American!

———————

Detroit didn't suit Nazar Panosian. He was grateful to be in the
United States. He appreciated his uncle's help. But this wasn't where
he wanted to start his new life. There was a large Armenian population
in Detroit, which was important to Nazar as to all Armenian immigrants. But there were other Armenian communities in other parts
of the country. He wanted less of a sprawling metropolis—truth be
told, something more like his hometown of Balan. And he wanted to
work in his own profession, making shoes, not taking the odd jobs his
uncle could help him acquire in Detroit. With his uncle's assistance,
Nazar settled on Binghamton, New York, where there was an Armenian settlement, and where there was also a large shoe manufacturer.
A few months after taking a train out of New York west to Detroit,
Nazar was backtracking. But this time, he had a plan.

Shortly after reaching Binghamton, Nazar found a job making
shoes. His employer was the Endicott-Johnson Shoe Factory, which
made Thom McAn shoes, among others. The company had been
founded in Binghamton in 1854. Eventually it spread to Johnson City
and Endicott—"the triple cities," two of which were conspicuously
named for the company's controlling partners. By 1920, Endicott-
Johnson was employing some twenty thousand people, and its treatment of its employees was ahead of its time. To avoid unionization, the
company provided employee benefits and contributed to community
projects—efforts that were part of what the visionary George F. Johnson called the "Square Deal." The company reached its climax in 1940,
supplying retailers in thirty states. It was Endicott-Johnson which
won the contracts to supply all footwear for the United States military
in World War I and World War II.

Nazar Panosian was a craftsman. He had been apprenticed in Turkey to make shoes—from start to finish. But in America, he was part

of an assembly line—a concept as American as baseball and apple pie. He no longer made shoes—he made *tongues* for shoes.

One might assume that a skilled cobbler like Nazar must have been insulted by the redundancy of the work. Instead, Dr. Panosian explained, he was thrilled by the ingeniousness of the production line and by the incentive to work hard for performance-based pay. When Dr. Panosian recalls his father's delight in his new job, he does so with all the enthusiasm of a ten-year-old bragging on his dad:

> My father would boast about "American ingenuity!" The magic of enterprise and initiative! Because it was piece work, he was to be paid by how much he could produce. This was thrilling: "The harder I work, the more I earn! What a country!"

Panosian laughs as he tells this story. He continues, speaking not of shoemaking, but of his father's profound patriotism: "My father is the only man I ever knew who was happy to pay income taxes. It meant that he was able to earn money in this country—in this *free* country!"

Panosian goes quiet for a moment, savoring the thought, then deadpans, "I never shared his eagerness to pay income tax."

Nazar's employment at Endicott-Johnson lasted less than one year. He worked hard—the only way he knew how to work, the way he worked when he was an apprentice, the way he worked when he was a shop owner in Balan. But his co-workers were unimpressed. Panosian explains:

> The foreman came to him and said, "Nazar, we can't pay you like this anymore. You're working too hard, making everybody else look bad. We have to end this arrangement." He was to be paid by the hour rather than by the piece. Well, my father was incensed! "You set the rules; I prospered under the rules; and now you want to *change* the rules. That's wrong! I quit!"

This was Nazar Panosian. He quit over the changed pay scale—over *principle*. He had moved to Binghamton specifically to work for this company, and it was a company known for its good treatment of its employees. But his conscience and innate sense of justice would not allow him to continue. Unfortunately, he didn't immediately find other employment, as most of the workforce in "the triple cities" worked for the company he had just left.

But Nazar Panosian had greater concerns than his next job.

On June 28, 1914, a world away in Sarajevo, Bosnia, a young Serbian nationalist named Gavrilo Princip assassinated the heir to the throne of the Austro-Hungarian Empire, Archduke Franz Ferdinand.

These people and places meant nothing to Nazar or to young men like him all over the world.

But the bullet fired by Princip hurled the world into the bloodiest war in modern history—the Great War, what we in hindsight call World War I.

To families around the world it would mean four terrible years of trench warfare, and seemingly innumerable casualties.

To Nazar, it would mean that the opportunity to bring his brother Manny to America had passed, at least for a time. There would be no transatlantic journeys for civilians during a world war.

To Manny and the other two million unsuspecting Armenians in Turkey, it set in motion the series of events that would crush them in a year's time.

CHAPTER FIFTEEN

"THE MURDER OF A NATION"

1915 — TURKEY

"My own Armenian nation
Is banished far away;
A godless, barbarous people
Dwells on my banks today."

—Raphael Patkanian[84]

"The Armenian massacre was the greatest crime of the war,
and failure to act against Turkey is to condone it; because
the failure to deal radically with the Turkish horror means
that all talk of guaranteeing the future peace of the world is
mischievous nonsense; and because when we now refuse to war
with Turkey we show that our announcement that we meant
'to make the world safe for democracy' was insincere claptrap."

—Theodore Roosevelt[85]

Devastating earthquakes are often preceded by smaller tremors, which seismologists call "foreshocks." Calm yields to calamity, which in turn yields to catastrophe.

---

[84] Raphael Patkanian's poem, "The Tears of Araxes," translated by Alice Stone Blackwell and Ohannes Chatschumian, tells of the sorrows of the personified Araxes (also called the Aras or Arax) River, which flows through Armenia. The story of the poem is told by Peter Balakian in *The Burning Tigris,* 18–19.

[85] This statement by former President Theodore Roosevelt was a jab at the current President, Woodrow Wilson, who had urged Congress to declare war on Germany in April 1917 in order "to make the world safe for democracy." It was written in a personal letter to Cleveland Hoadley Dodge on May 11, 1918.

As awful as Abdul Hamid II's terrors of 1895 were, they were only
the tremors before an even greater disaster befell the Turkish Armenians. The "earthquake" of the Armenian Genocide took place in 1915,
and by its conclusion, over one million Armenians—men, women, and
children—had been slaughtered.

For centuries, Turkish Muslims had hated their successful minority neighbors, the Christian Armenians. Their disdain was shown in
countless slights and persecutions, from insults and thefts to beatings and murders. But in April of 1915, the simmering prejudice and
hatred in Turkish hearts boiled over, called forth by Turkish leaders
who aimed at "the Turkification of Turkey"—a euphemism for the
extermination of non-Turks. The genocide wasn't just mob violence,
like that which had claimed the life of Sarkis Momjian in Antakya in
1910. It was official Turkish policy, the work of political and religious
leaders to excise once and for all "the cancerous Armenian tumor"
from the body of Turkey. Their aim, in the words of eyewitness Henry
Morgenthau, the American Ambassador to Turkey at the time, was
nothing short of "the murder of a nation."[86]

In many ways, Turkish rulers had proven to be inept, especially
when compared to their European neighbors. Turkey—"the Sick Man
of Europe"—was far behind European powers technologically and
economically. Turkey was backward, the laughingstock of the civilized
world—in part because Islam[87] had left its adherents in the Dark Ages
around the globe for centuries, and in part because of political corruption. The once mighty Ottoman Empire was losing power and territory with shocking regularity.

But their management of the Armenian Genocide was maniacally
masterful.

First, the Young Turks built their case against the Armenians.
They insisted that the Christians in their midst would aid and abet

---

[86] Morgenthau, *Ambassador Morgenthau's Story*, 203.
[87] Modern exceptions like Dubai and Qatar cannot disguise the fact that most Islamic nations
are decades and sometimes even centuries behind the rest of the world in their development.

the Christian nations which opposed Turkey in World War I—Russia, Great Britain, France, and eventually Italy. It is true that there were some Armenians who defected from northern Turkey to assist the Russians. Their hope was to liberate their countrymen. But most Armenians were loyal Turks; many even served in the Turkish army. Nevertheless, the loyalties of the entire Armenian population were called into question. The actions of a reckless few jeopardized the lives of millions. Armenians were already in the den of Turkish lions, and the rocks which revolutionaries threw at the lions only further awakened and enraged them.

In truth, supposed military threats were merely an excuse for the Turks to do what was already in their hearts.[88] They had learned from the failure of Hamid II in 1895 that it would be impossible to eradicate the Armenians during a time of peace. The smoke of war would provide them with the cover they needed to carry out their ghastly plans to eliminate the Armenians. While the world fought the Great War, Turkey committed the Great Crime.

Turkey's official entry into World War I as the ally of Germany and the enemy of the Allies was the final tremor before the "earthquake" of the 1915 genocide. Winning the war within her own borders against the Armenians took precedence even over the war against Russia, France, and Great Britain. Genocide survivor Grigoris Balakian describes the opportunistic Turks:

> The responsible and irresponsible leaders of the Turkish government believed that the world war was their sole opportunity, one unprecedented in the course of history, to destroy the Armenian people—the cancer destroying the Turkish empire. The countries of civilized Christian Europe were busy ripping one another apart, and Turkey's ally, Germany, was passive and silent in the matter.[89]

---

[88] John Keegan, writing in his book *The First World War,* concurs that the Armenian Genocide was completely unrelated to the war: "Awful though the Ottoman government's treatment of its Armenian subjects was, the forced marches organized to do them to death belong more properly to the history of the Ottoman imperial policy than to that of the war itself." John Keegan, *The First World War* (New York: Alfred A. Knopf, 1999), 8.

[89] Grigoris Balakian, *Armenian Golgotha,* 46.

They say that a man's character is revealed by what he does when no one is watching. Turkey's national character was revealed by what they did behind the cover of World War I. Ambassador Morgenthau's record is again insightful:

> For the first time in two centuries [Turks] could now live their national life according to their own inclinations, and govern their peoples according to their own will. The first expression of this rejuvenated national life was an episode which, so far as I know, is the most terrible in the history of the world. New Turkey, freed from European tutelage, celebrated its national rebirth by murdering not far from a million of its own subjects.[90]

The rationale of Turkish political leaders was bolstered by the rhetoric of Turkish religious leaders. Because they were Christians, Armenians were "infidels" who had to be exterminated in an Islamic *jihad*—a "holy war." In the words of Dr. Panosian, "It was essentially a religious conflict: Islam versus Christianity. And the Christian presence was an infection in the Muslim world." Historian Philip Jenkins concurs, explaining that the genocide was motivated by religion, not just race.

> The persecutions of 1915 might have begun with secular needs and the demands of military security, but once under way, the mobs and militias drew so freely on Islamic slogans and symbols that we are rather dealing with a popular religious or even apocalyptic movement. Muslim preachers stirred actions against Christians, particularly during Friday prayers, and incensed crowds gathered at mosques. Mobs used the war cry "Allahu Akbar!" and sought the forced conversions of Armenian Christians; they also destroyed or appropriated Christian buildings and institutions.[91]

Having stirred Turkey's Muslim majority to nationalistic fervor by portraying the Armenian Christians as a militaristic and religious threat to the nation, Turkish leaders began to carry out their appalling plans. Although their treatment of the Christians in their midst would eventually become shockingly barbaric, the Turks began the genocide with the precision of a surgeon.

---

[90] Morgenthau, *Ambassador Morgenthau's Story*, 258.
[91] Jenkins, *The Great and Holy War*, 304.

First, the Turks rid their own army of Armenian soldiers. In a time of national crisis—at the commencement of a world war—the Turks eliminated their own troops. G. J. Meyer explains: "They began in comparatively innocuous fashion, disarming their Armenian soldiers and assigning them to labor battalions. Then they proceeded to work, and starve, those battalions to death."[92]

Once the trained Armenian soldiers had been neutralized, the Turks disarmed the rest of the Armenian population, allegedly to prevent them from joining in the cause of the Allies. Occasionally, entire villages were disarmed in a show of equity, but the weapons of the Muslims were returned while the weapons of the Christians were kept. The Armenians were in a truly impossible position: those who gave up their firearms were punished for having them; those who said they had no firearms were accused of hiding them and punished more severely. The result of the confiscation of firearms was an unarmed minority—sheep in the midst of well-armed wolves.

The next step in the process was the arrest and deportation of Armenian leaders—church leaders, civil leaders, educators, and even poets. Armenians mark April 24, 1915, as the commencement of the genocide. On this date, beloved Armenian leaders were arrested throughout the Empire. They were deported, and once away from the eyes of the public, they were murdered.

Next, almost all Armenian men were deported throughout the Ottoman Empire. Sometimes it was under the pretext of being conscripted into the military. Sometimes they were taken on death marches to the interior of Turkey. Always they were taken away from their families. They almost never resisted, in part because they had no weapons, and in part because they hoped that their peaceful surrenders would prevent their wives and children from being harmed.

Able-bodied men were kept in prison camps—the precursors to German concentration camps—where they did grueling labor for the

---

[92] Meyer, *A World Undone*, 336.

Turkish war cause prior to their executions. The labor camps were hopeless places. The captives languished in intolerable conditions. Food and water were scarce. Lice were ubiquitous. Cold and damp living conditions inevitably led to disease. Typhoid claimed many. As one survivor of the devastating camps wrote, "There was no one left healthy who could bury the dead."[93]

Often, the men were tortured. The Ottomans were hellishly creative in their sadistic abuse of their Armenian countrymen, even studying methods of torture from the Spanish Inquisition. One Turkish governor had horseshoes nailed to the feet of Armenians and marched his victims through town to display his ingenuity and power.[94]

Among the Turks' favorite acts of cruelty was *bastinado*—the caning of the soles of their captives' bare feet. One victim's granddaughter records the result: "Afterward, the men's feet often resembled cooked sausages, swollen and split."[95] Such beatings sometimes resulted in amputations. Agonizingly, they often coincided with interminable marches.

On many occasions, the Turks would avoid even the pretense of a long deportation. Men were taken into the wilderness and immediately killed by their captors. The net effect of all of these efforts was the same across the tottering Empire. Armenians were disarmed. The disarmed men were deported. Armenian women, children, and the aged were left utterly defenseless.

The next stage in the masterplan of murder was the deportation of the entire Armenian population. Armenians were given only a day's notice that they were being forced to leave their homes with only what they could carry. They would try to sell their possessions to their Muslim neighbors, but everyone knew it was a farce, as their neighbors would plunder their possessions as soon as the Armenians were led out of town by military guards.

---

[93] Chorbadjian, *Surviving the Forgotten Armenian Genocide,* 11.
[94] Jenkins, *The Great and Holy War,* 301.
[95] MacKeen, *The Hundred-Year Walk,* 84.

This excerpt from *The Forty Days of Musa Dagh* describes the horrors of the forced evacuations—which were truly just extended exterminations:

> For many people it is depressing to relocate. A lost fragment of life always remains. To move to another town, settle in a foreign country, is for everyone a major decision. But, to be suddenly driven forth, within twenty-four hours, from one's home, one's work, the reward of years of steady industry. To become the helpless prey of hate. To be sent defenseless out on to Asiatic highroads, with several thousand miles of dust, stones, and morass before one. To know that one will never again find a decently human habitation, never again sit down to a proper table. Yet all this is nothing. To be more shackled than any convict. To be counted as outside the law, a vagabond, whom anyone has the right to kill unpunished. To be confined within a crawling herd of sick people, a moving concentration camp, in which no one is so much as allowed to ease his body without permission—who shall dare say he can measure the depths of anguish which invaded the minds of these people.[96]

Ambassador Morgenthau paints an equally horrific picture of the deportations:

> In a few days, what had been a procession of normal human beings became a stumbling horde of dust-covered skeletons, ravenously looking for scraps of food, eating any offal that came their way, crazed by the hideous sights that filled every hour of their existence, sick with all the diseases that accompany such hardships and privations, but still prodded on and on by the whips and clubs and bayonets of their executioners.[97]

The deportations were a vital part of the Turks' murderous strategy. They gave the Turkish leaders the possibility of denying the genocide. There were no "death marches," they would argue—only "relocations," a euphemism to cover their evil intentions. The ruse was that Armenians were being moved out of harm's way with the opportunity to resettle or to immigrate to other lands; the truth was that they were being driven to their deaths. Patrick Sookhdeo explains:

---

[96] Werfel, *The Forty Days of Musa Dagh*, 101.
[97] Morgenthau, *Ambassador Morgenthau's Story*, 212–213.

[In May of 1915] the scale of the deportation escalated dramatically, with the remaining Armenian population, mostly women and children, being sent to be settled in what the Ottoman authorities called "agricultural colonies." Their destinations were in fact barren areas without any provision of food, water or shelter, and it is clear that these deportees were not intended to survive. According to Ottoman records, 1.1 million were deported.[98]

Deniability was one goal of the deportations. Secrecy was another. The deportations allowed the gruesome murders of a million citizens to take place in the privacy of the wilderness, away from cities and witnesses. Dawn Anahid McKeen explains the shroud of secrecy: "With [the killings on April 24, 1915], the decimation of the Ottoman Armenian population had begun. Not with a thunderous roar from the Turkish majority but rather in secret, away from the population's gaze, in the ditches and back roads of the Ottoman Empire."[99]

The forced marches were indescribably miserable. All Armenians—including the elderly, the very young, and the sick—were forced to leave their homes, provisions, and most of their possessions. They were driven at gunpoint and motivated by whips. Turkish guards filled their pockets with the few treasures the Armenians carried with them. Armenians generally kept their savings in the form of gold jewelry. The Turks became fiendishly efficient at pillaging such treasures while ignoring what their captives easily jettisoned. Dr. Panosian explains:

> The Turks were crafty. They would empty a town of Armenians and tell them, "Take with you whatever you want." They would take them to a hill on the outskirts of the village, and they would insist that you "Run up the hill!" Now, you can't run with a suitcase. So you left— you just abandoned—whatever you couldn't carry. But some things you held closely. And the Turks would take whatever you had left at the *top* of the hill. They knew that was valuable. They didn't bother with the stuff they had left at the bottom.

Many Armenians would die en route, succumbing to the exhausting travel, the exposure to the elements, and the lack of nourishment.

---

[98] Sookhdeo, conclusion to *Surviving the Forgotten Armenian Genocide*, 107.
[99] MacKeen, *The Hundred-Year Walk*, 58.

Those unable to keep up, including children and the aged, were either left to die or dispatched with a single bullet. Sookhdeo again records harrowing details of the abuse:

> Walking barefoot over mountains and across the Der El-Zor desert with little or no food or water, the women and children were vulnerable to attack by their guards and by the local Kurds. They were soon robbed of anything they carried. Many were raped; many were killed. Many died of hunger, thirst and disease. The few remaining men were usually separated from the rest of the deportees and massacred. Hundreds of young women threw themselves into rivers or wells to drown; some drowned their babies too. Little girls were sold as wives to Kurdish ruffians. Some deportees were packed into cattle-trucks and sent to their doom by train. Others were kept alive for a while to work on extending the railway, women and children breaking stones and digging through the Taurus Mountains. Barely 20% of the deportees from this phase of deportation reached their destination.[100]

As if the danger of starvation, exhaustion, and disease weren't enough, Turkish authorities would release notoriously violent criminals, enlisting them as hired raiders to ambush the Armenians during their deportations. Grigoris Balakian, who experienced the torments firsthand, explains: "All the prisoners on death row, and all the convicts and criminals in the prisons of all the towns in Turkey, were to be pardoned and organized into bandit groups (*chetes*) to plunder and massacre the Armenian population without mercy, on the pretext of protecting the rear of the Ottoman army."[101]

Historian G. J. Meyer validates Balakian's description of the Turkish government's deployment of merciless *chetes:*

> In Constantinople thousands of convicted criminals were organized into death squads whose only assignment was to kill every Armenian they could find, giving first priority to those intellectuals, profession-

---

[100] Sookhdeo, conclusion to *Surviving the Forgotten Armenian Genocide,* 107. The region mentioned, "Der el-Zor" (also seen as "Deir el-Zor" or "Deir-ez-Zor") was the location of the largest concentration camps used by the Turks to contain and kill Armenians. Called "the epicenter of death" by Peter Balakian (*Burning Tigris,* 176), the region is the World War I equivalent of Auschwitz, the terrible Nazi concentration camp where Jews were slaughtered in World War II.

[101] Grigoris Balakian, *Armenian Golgotha,* 78.

als, and religious and political leaders who might have the potential to serve as leaders. The families of Turkish officials took the choicest booty; the death squads and rabble took the rest.[102]

The murderers were many, from trained soldiers to vicious *chetes* to a mob of bloodthirsty Muslims, including women. And the Turkish population turned a blind eye when attractive Armenian girls were raped or kidnapped and forced to convert to Islam. The conscience of the nation was at ease amid historic barbarism. Such cruelty to infidels was celebrated as a virtue rather than mourned as a vice. Philip Jenkins tells of the cruelty of rape, the "ravishing" (as it was called at the time) which became commonplace during the genocide:

> Rape has always been part of warfare, a predictable consequence of removing social restraints, but it had a special role in a society founded on principles of personal and family honor. Apart from gaining sexual advantage, perpetrators were also in effect destroying both those women and their families—and, by implication, shaming their religion and their race.[103]

More often than not, rape was followed by murder. By the end of 1915, central Turkey was a virtual graveyard. The gas chambers and crematoria of the Nazis were almost humane by comparison. A million Armenian bodies were left to rot on roads, in ravines, and in rivers and lakes throughout the interior of Turkey.

The weapons used to carry out the mass murders often included axes, machetes, and even garden hoes. Armenians were hacked to pieces to save bullets. They were burned to death. They were drowned. They were led into the mountains and forced to march off cliffs until literally thousands of bodies were piled in the canyons below.

The murderers made games of their grisly work. Children were thrown by horse-riding soldiers onto swords that had been buried in the ground, blade-up—the Turks' terrible "game of swords." Children were lined up in a row to see how many a single bullet could claim. Infants were cut from their mothers' wombs. Thousands were cruci-

---

[102] Meyer, *A World Undone*, 336.
[103] Jenkins, *The Great and Holy War*, 299.

fied in mockery of the Christian faith. Almost all were stripped naked before they were killed, as their Muslim murderers conscientiously avoided claiming clothing or jewelry from a dead body.

Witnesses who rode out to the killing zones tell of unimaginable horrors. Rivers were clogged with bodies. Roadsides were littered with corpses. Turkey literally stank of putrefaction and death.

Most Turks knew what was happening. Most, though not all, approved. But most were not forced to see the worst of it—again, thanks to the deportations. The Armenian Genocide was truly a hidden holocaust. Peter Balakian explains:

> The Turkish government used the severe and rocky terrain of Anatolia—with its cliffs, ravines, canyons, and gorges—to kill hundreds of thousands of Armenians and leave their corpses where they would be hidden from view.[104]

Grigoris Balakian's testimony records orders which were sent to a local Ottoman leader, detailing both the desired atrocity and secrecy: "Without mercy and without pity, kill all from the one-month-old to the ninety-year-old, but see to it that this massacre is not conducted in the towns and in the presence of the people."[105]

Sultan Abdul Hamid II was called "The Bloody Sultan" as a result of the atrocities he authorized in 1895. But the Young Turks who replaced him, promising democracy and ethnic unity, more than tripled his crimes against the Armenians. The Turkish population at the beginning of 1915 was around thirty million. By the end of the year, one million of them—the majority of the peaceful Armenian population—had been savagely and methodically slaughtered, without conscience or remorse. Talaat Pasha, the strongest man in Turkey during the genocide of 1915, bragged to American Ambassador Henry

---

[104] Peter Balkanian, introduction to *Armenia's Golgotha*, trans. Peter Balakian with Aris Sevag (New York: Vintage Books, 2009), xxv.
[105] Grigoris Balakian, *Armenian Golgotha*, 79.

Morgenthau, "I have accomplished more toward the solving of the Armenian problem in three months than Abdul Hamid accomplished in thirty years!"[106]

Talaat Pasha's boasting about his murderous exploits is disgusting. But the efforts of modern Turkey to cover up the crimes of their forebears are no less so. To this day, the Armenian Genocide is denied by Turkey. They minimize the deaths of Armenians, dismissing them as a necessary response to Armenian rebellion. They claim—against all evidence—that the genocide is merely a fabrication of bitter Armenians and hateful Europeans. They have added the crime of denial to the crime of ethnic cleansing. The genocide has been minimized additionally by the United States government, which has refused even to use the term "genocide" to describe the massacres lest it offend the leaders of Turkey, a valued ally in modern times. Best-selling historian G. J. Meyer explains:

> No one would ever be punished. In the years after the war the United States found it more advantageous to come to terms with the Muslims of the Middle East with their oil riches than to redress the wrongs done to [the] Armenian nation. . . . Successive Turkish governments continued into the twenty-first century not only to deny that an Armenian genocide ever occurred but to prosecute any Turk who dared to write of it.[107]

The Armenian Genocide was too quickly forgotten. By the Great War's end, even the victors were too fatigued to ensure reparations for the persecuted Armenians. A great crime had been committed, but little was done to prosecute the criminals. As a result, the Armenian Genocide was the first of the blood-soaked twentieth century, not the last. The failure of the civilized world to adequately respond to Turkey's treachery left the door open to ethnic cleansing in the future. The unthinkable had become possible. The Armenian Genocide was "the template for most of the genocide that followed in the twentieth century."[108]

---

[106] Morgenthau, *Ambassador Morgenthau's Story,* 229.
[107] Meyer, *A World Undone,* 337.
[108] Peter Balakian, introduction to *Armenian Golgotha,* xiv.

Dr. Panosian retells a story of Hitler's allusion to the Armenian Genocide:

> When he was contemplating the genocide against the Jews, one brave subordinate is supposed to have said, "But Führer, this will write your name in infamy!" And he is supposed to have replied, disdainfully, "Who remembers the Armenians?" And he was right. Most people have never heard this story. Most people know nothing about this.

Ambassador Henry Morgenthau called the acts of Turkey against the Armenians "the most terrible in the history of the world." His use of such superlative language is powerful.[109] Elsewhere in his memoirs, he writes, "I am confident that the whole history of the human race contains no such horrible episode as this."[110]

He was probably correct. But not for long. Tragically—and ironically, since Morgenthau himself was a Jew—the Turks would hold the dubious honor of committing history's worst crime for fewer than thirty years. Within Morgenthau's own lifetime (he died in 1946), Hitler would outdistance the abominations even of Turkey in his slaughter of the Jews. Germany—who tacitly looked on and at times even defended the Armenian Genocide—learned from their less sophisticated allies.

- They learned that deportation was a viable excuse to uproot a minority and move them to isolated locations for their extermination.
- They learned that ethnic cleansing galvanizes citizens. Racism stirs nationalism to a fever pitch.
- They learned that an extensive war creates a diversion which makes the murder of millions possible.
- They learned to stomach vile acts for the sake of "victory at any price."
- They learned that atrocities committed during a world war will be ignored during the war and forgotten soon afterward.

---

[109] Morgenthau, *Ambassador Morgenthau's Story*, 186.
[110] Morgenthau, *Ambassador Morgenthau's Story*, 216.

In part because Turkey got away with murder—and has been allowed for a full century to deny that it even happened—the human race now contains several "such horrible episode[s] as this." The final casualties of the Armenian Genocide and the world's failure to address it were the Jews of World War II, the Ukrainians of Stalin's Russia, the peasants of Cambodia, the Tutsis of Rwanda, and millions more who have died under the banner of ethnic cleansing since Turkey first introduced the concept to a pitying but passive world.

Contrary to Turkey's century-long cover-up, the Armenian Genocide happened. It was unprovoked. It was a well-developed and carefully executed plan to rid the Ottoman Empire of its most successful citizens, the minority they described as "vermin" and a "cancer" in their midst. By the end of the genocide, 1.5 million Armenians had been murdered in one of the most heinous crimes in human history.

Among the multitudes who were slain was Manuel Panosian, Nazar's younger brother.

PART FOUR

"IN PATHS OF RIGHTEOUSNESS"

CHAPTER SIXTEEN

TREASURE HUNT

1919 — BEIRUT, LEBANON

"For whatsoever from one place doth fall,
Is with the tide unto another brought:
For there is nothing lost, that may be found, if sought."

—Edmund Spenser[111]

Beirut, Lebanon. To the modern mind, the very mention of the city stirs images of political upheaval, racial strife, and civil war. Deservedly so. Lebanon has dealt with racial and religious tensions throughout its storied history. William Harris, a student of Lebanon's past and present, describes it as "a conglomerate of Christian, Muslim, and Muslim-derived communal minorities, with distinctive identities, legal personalities, and political representation."[112] At times, the demographic parity has led to an uneasy peace. At other times, as in the civil warfare that erupted in 1975, it has led to brutality and bloodshed.

Ironically, a century ago, Beirut was a place of *safety*—a lifeboat amidst an ocean of chaos. World War I, optimistically dubbed "The War to End All Wars" at the time, was the bloodiest war in history. By its conclusion, over eight million soldiers had been killed. An estimated thirteen million more civilians eventually lost their lives to the disease and starvation that followed the war.[113]

---

[111] Edmund Spenser, *The Faerie Queene*, V.ii.39.9. https://scholarsbank.uoregon.edu/xmlui/bitstream/handle/1794/784/faeriequeene.pdf. Accessed Aug. 27, 2018.

[112] William Harris, *Lebanon: A History, 600–2001* (Oxford, England: Oxford University Press, 2012), 3.

[113] John Graham Royde-Smith, "World War I: Killed, Wounded, and Missing," *Encyclopedia Britannica*, www.britannica.com/event/World-War-I/Killed-wounded-and-missing. Accessed Aug. 27, 2018.

The Armistice signed on November 11, 1918, may have ended the hostilities between Germany and the Allies, but it did not fix the world which the war had shattered.[114] Nothing was the same. Millions had died. Borders had moved. Families, like the Momjians, had been irreparably broken.

Beirut swelled during the war, bulging with missionaries, refugees, and orphans. Whereas its population was around seventy thousand in 1860, it had ballooned to over one hundred fifty thousand in 1914, due in large part to refugees.[115] Beirut scholar Samir Kassir estimates that there were twenty-eight thousand Armenian and Syrian Christian refugees in the ancient city by 1920.[116] Somehow the "Beirut lifeboat" remained afloat. How had it avoided the ubiquitous and rampant bloodshed around it? Politics and providence.

Beirut is one of the oldest cities in the world, boasting a history that traces back more than five thousand years. After its conquest by Sultan Salim I in 1516, Lebanon was part of the expansive Ottoman Empire. But during the nineteenth century, Lebanon came under the financial patronage of France and other European powers. While some Ottomans may have objected to French influence, all were grateful for French investments: by the beginning of the twentieth century, French engineers had turned Beirut into an important port on the Mediterranean. French developers had helped build modern roads—perhaps the very roads that in God's providence brought the three youngest Momjian children to safety during their flight from Antakya in 1910.

Christian missionaries from all over Europe had made Beirut a headquarters of western missions. Samir Kassir explains:

> Beirut . . . occupied a special position by virtue of its status as a bridgehead of European economic expansion, and therefore a place where everyone wished to be represented. Hence the concentration of missions from all denominations and the appearance of institutions at all levels.[117]

---

[114] By a happy coincidence, Armistice Day, November 11, is the birthday of Nazar Panosian.
[115] William Harris, *Lebanon*, 168.
[116] Kassir, *Beirut*, 268.
[117] Kassir, *Beirut*, 179.

French investors had made Beirut one of the financial capitals of the Middle East. Its citizens longed to be "modern." It was a liberal city that embraced the Ottoman Tanzimat Reform Acts of 1839 and 1856 that called for citizens of all faiths and nationalities to be treated as equals. Its leaders believed that "modernization was the sole road to salvation" and that "the equality of subjects before the law favored a city that was prepared to move forward."[118] Beirut was an Ottoman city *politically*, but it had French interests *economically*. It was valued by both sides of World War I. As a result, both sides left it alone. War raged nearby, but Beirut was untouched. Consequently, refugees, educators, and missionaries rushed in.

———

In 1918, by the war's end, Emma Momjian had been in the United States for eight long years. She had heard nothing of her three youngest children since she had left them in the care of German missionaries before sailing to the United States. She hadn't expected to hear from them. That part of the world—the place where she had left her beloved children—was in upheaval. And they had been so young. Sara had been eight, Rose six, and Mihran just four. Her heart broke to think of it.

Despite the loss of everything she held dear, Emma carved out a new life in America. Her Armenian neighbors gave her at least a semblance of connection to happier times. She appreciated the close-knit Armenian community, which centered in the Armenian Apostolic Church. Panosian explains: "Interestingly, the church was the institution that kept the Armenians together. It was maintained in their national language. It was the place of social concourse. The social institution was the church."[119]

---

[118] Kassir, *Beirut*, 131.

[119] Historian Francis Whiting Halsey concurs: "Nearly a thousand years have gone by since the fall of the last definite political state of the Armenians, but their church has held them in national consciousness and preserved in them distinguishing racial and social characteristics. The Church is more than religion to the Armenian; it is his patriotism, his hope for survival, and the banner under which he rallies for his people" (*The Literary Digest History of the World War*, 38–39). Halsey wrote in 1919, over seventy years before the founding of the modern Republic of Armenia in 1991.

Emma was also grateful for her Uncle Dick's generosity, but she refused to be a burden on him. Determined to make her own way, she found work as the matron of a boarding house in Binghamton, New York, serving as a landlady, cook, and housekeeper for Armenian tenants. It was a job which met her material needs—and would one day do much more.

———————

America's entry into World War I had hastened the war's end. By 1919, for the first time in over five years, transatlantic trips were again possible. Returning to the Middle East was perhaps safe, even for an Armenian. Thus, Emma determined to go hunt for her lost children. She had no real reason to believe they had survived the war. The atrocities of 1910 that took her husband's life and scattered the rest of her family had been only the beginning. The Armenian Genocide had ravaged Turkey throughout 1915. Like everyone else in the West, Emma read harrowing newspaper reports of the murder of over one million Armenians in her homeland. While the news was heartbreaking to all Americans, it was infinitely worse for her. Were her children included in the staggering number of martyrs? Had they escaped with the German missionaries to Beirut? Were they living or dead? She had no answers, but she couldn't rest until she did.

Emma told her uncle, Dick Davidian, of her intention to return to Turkey, or at least to Lebanon, the safe harbor to which the German missionaries had intended to take her three children eight years earlier. But for those eight years Davidian had cared for Emma as if she were his own daughter. He would not hear of her going to the war-torn Middle East. He was old-fashioned and chivalrous. He himself would go in her place. He would search for his great-nephew and nieces, hopeless as it seemed. He didn't voice his doubts to her. Instead, he made plans to sail for Beirut as soon as possible—doing so before the calendar had turned to 1920, embarking on a treasure hunt like no other.

———————

Like everyone else, the Deaconess was relieved that the war had ended. But for the orphans under her care in the evangelical German orphanage in Beirut, it made little difference. Most of them were with her because their parents had been killed, either in the war or in the genocide that used the war as a cover. A few parents like Emma had sent their children to safety, away from the reach of Turkish mobs and soldiers. But most of those parents had succumbed to the very threats from which they were protecting their children. No one came looking to reclaim the orphans under her care.

But one day someone did.

Dick Davidian must have been struck by the beauty of Beirut, situated strikingly between the Mediterranean Sea and the Lebanon Mountains. Especially noteworthy are the seaside cliffs and the majestic Pigeon Rocks, which jut out of the sea just a stone's throw from the shore, looking very much like stone sentinels protecting the city.[120]

But Davidian was no tourist. He arrived in Beirut with an enormous task. He was looking for children he had never met. By the time he set foot in Lebanon, nine years had passed since Emma had entrusted her three children to German missionaries. During those nine years the Great War and the Armenian Genocide had turned the entire world upside down. He had no idea whether the children were still alive, much less in Beirut. He could only find out by scouring the ancient city, asking about German orphanages and Armenian refugees.

In a remarkable display of God's grace, his quest was successful. He did find the German orphanages, and he did find his nieces and nephew. Countless orphans had perished during the war, but the Momjians were not among them. His was the joy of Abraham's steward, whose discovery of Abraham's family in distant Nahor could be explained not by good fortune, but only by the goodness of God in

---

[120] At the beginning of the twentieth century, Beirut was a beautiful city, a combination of the sophistication of Paris and the mysteries of the Middle East. In his classic novel *The Forty Days of Musa Dagh*, Franz Werfel wrote that "no landscape on earth has greater charms" (8). However, urban sprawl and civil war have almost entirely hidden the city's "charms" today, burying them under concrete.

directing his steps.[121] Well might he have repurposed the thanksgiving in Genesis 24:48 to rejoice in another astounding and providential discovery, almost four millennia later: "And I bowed down my head, and worshipped the LORD, and blessed the LORD God of my niece Emma, which had led me in the right way to take my niece's children unto her."

What were the chances of finding these three needles in the smoldering haystack of the post-war Middle East? As unlikely as it was, he had indeed found them! His prayers had been answered!

The Deaconess' heart must have beat quickly as she walked to find Sara and tell her the news. This kind woman had witnessed so much tragedy, and she had surely learned to steel herself against sentimental emotions. But days like this—*outcomes* like this—were all too rare, almost impossible! Tears of joy and sorrow must have flowed. She had succeeded in caring for some of the most vulnerable people in the world. And her success now required her to say goodbye to children she had treated as her own for nine years.

The three Momjian children boarded the great ship with the uncle they had only recently met. They sailed toward a country they had never dared to imagine. They sailed to a mother whom they could barely remember. And yet they knew they were uniquely blessed.

Dr. Panosian tells of their journey: "They sailed from Beirut. They went to Marseille, France. And they sailed from Marseille on one of the first American troop ships bringing American soldiers back from Europe, in 1919."

What a change, especially for Sara and Rose, ages seventeen and fifteen, respectively. They had spent the last nine years surrounded by children and deaconesses—Protestant nuns, for all practical purposes. Now they were surrounded by young American soldiers, "many of them teenagers who hadn't seen girls in a long time," Dr. Panosian points out. Sara was shy, and she barely dared to look the Americans in the

----

[121] Genesis 24.

eye. Rose was anything but shy. Throughout her life, Sara would talk about the scandal of her audacious younger sister vying for the soldiers' attention aboard that ship: "She *flirted* with them! The *entire* trip!" Fortunately for the girls—and to the chagrin of more than a few young men—the girls' Uncle Dick "could not have been more solicitous of the girls' well-being on the ship," in Panosian's words. They were his responsibility, and he was as determined as if he were engaged in his own personal trench warfare. His motto echoed that of the French army, which World War I veteran J. R. R. Tolkien would later put on the lips of Gandalf: "You shall not pass!"

Uncle Dick returned to his home in Binghamton, New York, with three wide-eyed parcels. He delivered them to their mother, then slipped away so they could enjoy their reunion in private. "Imagine what that reunion must have meant," Panosian says. Nine years had passed since they were last together. Emma welcomed the children she had left behind, embracing them, uttering prayers of thankfulness, and sobbing much as she had when she had left them.

Emma Momjian's decision to leave her children with strangers—the most excruciating choice of her life—was vindicated. She and her children had witnessed and endured appalling things. But they had survived. And although she desperately missed her husband, she rejoiced at the goodness and providence of God that had brought her children home—orphans no more.

"This is the LORD's doing; it is marvelous in our eyes."[122]

---

[122] Psalm 118:23 KJV.

Immigration group, 1919; Sara Momjian is in the back row, second from the left

CHAPTER SEVENTEEN

THE AMERICAN DREAM

1917–1921 — BINGHAMTON, NEW YORK
FORT DIX, NEW JERSEY
AND ELMIRA, NEW YORK

"Lord, we tank Tee for our Savior.
We tank Tee for our family.
And we tank Tee for our country!"

—Nazar Panosian

On April 6, 1917, the United States entered The Great War, joining the Allies (Great Britain, France, and Italy, as Russia had already surrendered) and declaring war on Germany. America's intent, in the words of President Woodrow Wilson, was to "make the world safe for democracy." Like Japan's attack on Pearl Harbor in World War II, Germany's sinking of American ships and scheming to incite war between Mexico and the United States awakened a sleeping giant. America, which had been determined to sit out the war and maintain its neutrality, was called to action.

Nazar enlisted. Retrieving Manny from Turkey was impossible until the war's conclusion, so he joined the cause. His purpose was twofold: to support his new homeland in their war against the murderous Turks and Germans, and thereby to expedite his own American citizenship. Panosian explains:

> As an alien, Dad was not required to enlist as part of the draft. But if he volunteered, it would accelerate the process of his becoming a citizen, which he was so eager to do. Conversely, if he did not volunteer, it might hinder the process.

Just over one hundred sixteen thousand American soldiers died in World War I. Nazar was not among them. By the grace of God, the closest he got to the frontlines was the chow line in Fort Dix, NJ, where he served as a cook until the war's completion.

During his service at Fort Dix, Nazar did become the hero of a humorous "war story." As part of the war effort, local citizens would often invite soldiers serving at Fort Dix to join them for Sunday dinner, just to give them a taste of home. Nazar came regularly to one family's home. It turns out that one of the young ladies in that family had an eye for Private Panosian, though he probably never knew it. Her secret came out two generations later. Dr. Panosian picks up the story:

> Out of the clear blue sky a young girl came up to me after a History of Civ class one day and said, "I know something that you don't know! My great-grandmother had a crush on your father!" Her family had been the ones who had hosted my father so many years before! If he had reciprocated, I would never have come to be! And I wouldn't have this nose, either!

Discharged from the military at the war's end, Nazar returned to Binghamton in 1918. As expected, he looked for housing among the Armenian population gathered in the city. He found it at a boarding house which was managed by a middle-aged Armenian widow. Like all the Armenians Nazar had met, her story was one of deep sorrow. She had lost everything to the Turks. He understood, and he grieved for her.

Several months after his return to Binghamton, the boarding house tenants—along with the entire Armenian community—were astonished by the most improbable news. The quiet landlady, Emma Momjian, had news from Beirut, Lebanon. Her uncle had gone there on a fool's errand, searching for her three young children, last seen in Turkey. Nine years—and the terrible genocide—had transpired since their parting. But amazingly, he had found them, and they were coming to Binghamton! The Armenians rejoiced as though Emma's children were their own. They had shared each other's sorrows, and they now shared each other's joys.

Sara, Rose, and Mihran Momjian were reunited with their mother and their brother James, who had come to America with his mother in

1910.[123] The three miracle refugees were celebrities in the Armenian cluster in Binghamton. Almost no one survived the genocide—even adults. But these children *did!* America was a great adjustment to them, but their extended Armenian family helped. Mihran was thirteen, and he enrolled in school, despite his inability to speak English.[124] Sara was seventeen, and Rose was fifteen.[125] They were nearly grown, so they began to work with their mother in the boarding house rather than attending school.

Nazar noticed Sara immediately. She was younger by nine years. But even at seventeen, she was a lady, he thought to himself. He observed her whenever he had the opportunity. She was beautiful. She was kind. She cooked. She kept house. She managed even more efficiently than her mother—the result of serving countless children for nine years in a German orphanage. And unlike her sister, she blushed in front of men. He liked that. Best of all, she was an Armenian. Dr. Panosian speaks of his father's romantic interests: "He wanted an Armenian. He *needed* an Armenian because he needed the food, he needed the language, and so forth."

Nazar began making conversation with her. Though quiet, she returned his kind attention. There was hope! But he knew if he intended to win her, he would need to prove himself. He wanted to show her—and to show her protective mother and great-uncle—that he was worthy of her. He made a plan, and he spent the next two years carrying it out.

No more working for others, he thought. That had ended badly at the shoe factory. Nazar longed for the freedom to build his own shoe

---

[123] James Momjian never fully recovered from the injury he sustained at the hands of the Turks on the day when they kicked him aside and killed his father in Antakya, Turkey. He lived to see his three younger siblings again, but he passed away in 1922, at the age of twenty-three. (myheritage.com/names/james_momjian)

[124] Dr. Panosian's Uncle Mihran spent his adult years in Long Island, where he had a career as a photo engraver. He married an Armenian lady and had children—Dr. Panosian's cousins. He eventually settled in Florida, where he was converted listening to preaching from Pensacola Christian College—a trophy of God's grace!

[125] Dr. Panosian's Aunt Rose married an Armenian man and moved to California, where she spent the rest of her life. In her widowhood, Emma Momjian would spend half the year with Sara in New York and half with Rose in California. She lived with her daughters until her death.

business as he had in Balan, Turkey. But he had been around Binghamton long enough to know that he could not compete with the behemoth Endicott-Johnson Shoe Factory. He researched the neighboring communities and settled on Elmira, New York. It was sixty miles west of Binghamton—far enough to avoid competition with E-J Shoes, but close enough to be near Sara's family. Elmira would be his home—and unknown to him, the home of his posterity for the next century.

In the providence of God, the move to Elmira was also a move away from the Armenian Apostolic Church. There were only five or six Armenian families in Elmira—enough for regular gatherings, complete with backgammon games always, but not enough for a church. As a result, Nazar began to attend evangelical churches where the gospel was preached, including a Christian Missionary Alliance church and a Baptist church.

In 1919 Nazar Panosian founded a shoe repair shop in Elmira, New York. He proudly called it "South Main Street Shoe Repair." It would later be renamed "Panosian's Shoes."

Sara & Nazar Panosian in their South Main Street Shoe Repair shop, 1920

And in 1921 Nazar Panosian married Sara Momjian. Both had narrowly escaped Turkey. Both had lost loved ones to the genocide. And now both were intent on building a life in America together.

An amazing part of Sara's story is that she survived the tragedies in Turkey with not only her life intact, but her innocence. While thousands of Armenian girls had been raped, Sara had escaped unharmed. She wed with complete naïveté about what Proverbs 30:19 calls "the way of a man with a maid." God had been remarkably good.

In less than two years, Sara had gone from being an orphan in Beirut—a girl with no parents, no possessions, and no prospects—to owning a small business in the United States alongside her husband. In the words of her husband, "What a country!"

Nazar's unrivaled work ethic and integrity had served him well in Balan, Turkey. It served him well in Elmira, New York, too. He started a shoe repair shop, leaving manufacturing to the American assembly lines. But he became frustrated by the poor quality of the shoes his customers would bring in for repair, and he would urge them, "Buy your family some *quality* shoes!" His customers would reply, "*Where, Nazar?*" Soon he was selling shoes in addition to repairing them. The shoemaker-turned-shoe-repairer found his niche as a shoe seller. He and Sara bought property around their small shop and enlarged the store several times.

The growth of their family kept pace with the growth of their business. Two years into their marriage, they welcomed their first son. Manuel Panosian was born on May 2, 1922. He was named in honor of Nazar's brother, who, to Nazar's great grief, had never made it out of Turkey. Fifteen months later, they added baby James on August 16, 1923. James was named in honor of Emma's brother, who had died in America as a young adult.

Three more children were added in the next several years: Ruth on March 5, 1927; Edward on August 19, 1930; Stanley on August 25, 1939. Of the five children, three were born in August—a fact which the family always attributed to the cold New York Novembers!

Dr. Panosian remembers the tireless labors of his father. His mother would bring lunch to the shop, and they would eat together for just a few moments before she returned home and he returned to work. Their lives were full, but not easy:

> Dad's hands are rough—and dirty. His apron is dirty. Dad comes home, and they're washing diapers by hand in the bath tub. Dad is helping. His hands are weathered, and now they are being softened and becoming chapped. And he has to re-weather them when he goes back to his bench. It was hardship. This was their life.

Nazar's unbending integrity sometimes manifested itself in comical ways. He would raise the price on new inventory by a consistent amount, perhaps $1.00 per pair of shoes. So a pair of shoes which cost him $3.00 would sell for $4.00. The same exact model of shoe might arrive in a later shipment and cost Nazar $3.50. Instead of raising his prices overall as some might do, he would add $1.00 to the price of that $3.50 pair of shoes and put them on the shelf for $4.50, right next to the identical pair which still sold for $4.00. Friends would tell him, "Nazar, this is no way to do business! You can't sell identical pairs of shoes for $4.00 and $4.50!" Panosian recalls his father's answer, with both amusement and admiration:

> He would say, "These Americans! They *want* you to cheat them! The first shipment of shoes did not cost *me* more. Why should I charge *my customers* more? America!" That's my dad! [He laughs loudly, then collects himself to make a serious observation.] But it was integrity, it was honesty, it was character to him, to not raise the price on shoes he had purchased earlier for less.

In another conversation, Dr. Panosian summarized his father's character in a similar way: "Throughout his life, he was fiercely principled and honest, and he could not tolerate or even understand those who lacked basic integrity."[126]

---

[126] Nazar Panosian's passion for principle was passed on to his son. My friend Joe Tyrpak recalls a powerful lesson from Dr. Panosian on politics: "Polls make politicians; principles make statesmen. For a politician, the next election determines his decisions. For a statesman, the next generation determines his decisions. Republics don't usually last longer than two hundred years. They aren't conquered from without; they're termite-eaten from within."

But Panosian's Shoes was remarkably successful. From a startup in a tiny shop, the company thrived, at one point boasting thirteen stores in central New York and northern Pennsylvania and employing over one hundred people.[127] Students would approach Dr. Panosian years later in History of Civ at BJU and tell him, "I know the Panosian name! We used to go there to buy shoes!"

Dr. Panosian speaks of his father with a sense of wonder: "He didn't know English when he arrived in America. He had the equivalent of a third-grade education, and he made a success in America, and he established a godly home."

He also recalls his father's simple and profound prayers:

> He would pray, in his thick accent, the same three words of thanksgiving: "Lord, we *tank* Tee for our Savior. We *tank* Tee for our family. And we *tank* Tee for our country!" And we never wondered what country he meant by "our country." My dad was an American! His country was America! "The land of the free!" It was a privilege to work hard and to prosper.

Nazar and Sara Panosian were so eager to fit into their new homeland that they never spoke Armenian in their home, except perhaps when they were talking with each other about the children. "We knew that was a time to hide," Panosian recalls with mock fear. The results of their constant labors to master English were twofold: they learned English, and their children never learned Armenian—something Dr. Panosian regrets but understands.

Panosian ends his commentary on his father's success with the sorrow that is ubiquitous to every Armenian family. War broke out shortly after Nazar's immigration to the United States, precluding any opportunity to bring his younger brother to the United States. The fact that he lived and his brother died haunted him for his entire life.

> It was always a regret of my father's, and a reason my father named his firstborn son after his brother Manuel. It wasn't his fault. But he always regretted it. Dad felt almost . . . responsible that he had been

[127] Jeffrey Aaron, "Service Saturday for Elmira Businessman Manny Panosian," *Star Gazette* (Elmira, NY), Jan. 28, 2015.

the fortunate one. He almost regretted that, at the expense of his brother, he had come.

The life of the typical Armenian is intentional, principled, and joyful. But wherever there is memory of the genocide, there is grief mingled with gratitude.

CHAPTER EIGHTEEN

BOYHOOD

1 9 3 7 – 1 9 4 7 — ELMIRA, NEW YORK

*"Habits, like trees, are strengthened by age. A boy may
bend an oak, when it is a sapling—a hundred men
cannot root it up, when it is a full-grown tree."*

—J. C. Ryle[128]

For some former students and acquaintances, it may be hard to
think of Dr. Panosian—the one so often called upon to portray "the
voice of God"—as a boy. It's not difficult for me, thanks to a church
service in Greenville, South Carolina, in 1997. I arrived just before a
Sunday evening service at Hampton Park Baptist Church. Because
of my late arrival, I had to sit in the balcony, where I chanced to sit
beside my esteemed Church History professor. The guest speaker in
the service was an evangelist who performed "gospel magic"—"gospel
illusions" if you find the reference to the dark arts offensive. The man
would set up a trick, teach a scriptural lesson while he had the congregation's rapt attention, then finally complete the trick: turning a
red handkerchief white, joining cut pieces of rope into a single whole,
or the like. Throughout the performance, Dr. Panosian couldn't resist
leaning forward and craning his neck from side to side to obtain a
better view. He would smile at the jokes and show wonder on his face
during the tricks. It occurred to me that the respected professor, in his
sixties at the time, was really a boy at heart.

---

[128] J. C. Ryle, *Thoughts for Young Men* (Edinburgh, UK: Banner of Truth Trust, 2016), 11.

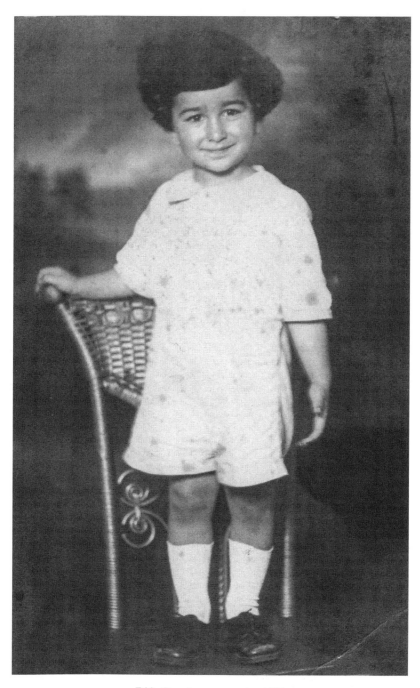

Eddie Panosian, age two, circa 1933

Dr. Panosian was born in 1930, so he grew up through the Great Depression. His family was not wealthy, but he and his four siblings were always provided for. His father worked hard to meet their needs. Contrary to the proverb, the cobbler's kids did have shoes—two pairs, in fact. And leather shoes, never tennis shoes.

I noted during one of our conversations that Dr. Panosian speaks with unmistakable warmth whenever his father is mentioned. I asked him why. He began with a short answer: "He was a disciplined figure. I feared his wrath."

At that point, I noticed that he was debating with himself about whether he should tell me a particular story about his father. Ultimately, he decided to share it, although he was uncertain that it should be included in this book. "But it tells you something about him," he reasoned. What he shared is my favorite memory of our time together, and I insisted that it be included in this biography. Dr. Panosian tells it far better than I could, so I'll let him. Hear his deliberate cadence and dramatic expression.

> We didn't have school buses in those days. We walked to school. It was not a hardship. It was just four or five blocks from my home to my school.
>
> On the way to my elementary school, as I am six or seven years old—I don't remember exactly how old I was—I passed a candy store. It had school supplies and so forth, but to me it was a candy store. Penny candy was *something* in those days. You got a good deal of candy for two or three pennies. Now, I don't know how this started—I honestly *don't know* how this started. But I discovered that I could steal some coins from my mother's purse. And with those coins I could buy candy. And with that candy I could make friends at school. I could *buy* friendship. [He laughs at seven-year-old Ed.]
>
> This led to a memorable experience that I have never forgotten. [This time his voice wells up with a far deeper emotion. The memory is clearly one of the most precious of his life.]
>
> My dad was to be obeyed. His wrath was controlled . . . but . . . *memorable.*
>
> Eventually, after I had been snitching coins for I don't know how long, my mother discovered what I had been doing and confronted me.

[The tension in the room was thick as I listened to him, and I couldn't help but laugh out and exclaim, "I love this story! I don't even know how it's going to end, but I love it!" I finally managed to stop snickering and asked him to continue. I was in for a surprise.]

She confronted me one afternoon. "Edvert? Edvert?" That's the way she pronounced my name. "Edvert? Have you been taking money from my purse?" I admitted it. It had been found out, and I couldn't hide it. I don't remember what she said, except that we got down on our knees in front of the old sofa in the living room. I prayed and she prayed that the Lord would forgive me. I got up, and I was happy. It had been settled! It was all over!

And then she said, "Now, we must tell Dad—we must tell Daddy about this." And now my whole life fled before me. "No, Mom!" I said. "Yes," she replied. "He'll want to know. And he loves you, too. He'll want to know." My momentary calm was now driven to disaster.

I don't remember how many days later, but within the same week, after supper, my mother and my siblings all went to visit a neighbor. Dad and I were left home alone. He had been informed, but he hadn't said a word about it yet. I suspect that he and Mom had arranged that she would leave with the others.

We heated in those days with a coal-fired furnace, and Dad had in the basement a bin of wood leftovers—short pieces of finished wood that remained from furniture projects. Dad used the scraps for kindling to start the fire in the morning. I had often worked with Dad on projects. He let me bring his tools and watch him, and assist him, and hand him tools, and so forth. After supper, when Mother and my siblings had left, he said, "Edvert?" He said, "Go downstairs and find a piece of wood." He told me the approximate length, and I was glad to do it. I wasn't suspecting anything, although I was surprised he didn't ask me to get any tools. I figured he had a project in mind. I'm oblivious to his intent. I bring the piece of wood up—perhaps one inch by two inches, and about eighteen inches long. He looked at it and said, "Good." Then he said, "Now, let's go upstairs."

We went upstairs to my room. I didn't have tools. I had this piece of wood. He sits down alongside my bed—I can see this now, seventy years later. . . . *eighty* years later, I can see this clearly! He says, "Sit here, Edvert." And then he said, "Edvert, Mother told me what you have done." I groaned. Here I thought we've gotten over the hump, and we have a project. As it turns out, Dad's project wasn't what I expected. *I* was the project! I thought, "Uh-oh. Here it comes."

Then he said, "Now I'm going to kneel by your bed. And I want you to take this wood. And I want you to strike me on my back with it, as hard as you can."

"No! No! Dad, I can't!" I say. This is my father!

"Yes, yes!"

And so timidly I—I *strike* my father.

He says, "Do it again! Harder!" And I'm dissolving into tears. And I hit my father again. "Again!" he said.

Finally, I don't remember after how many blows, he said, "That's enough. That's enough."

Then he slowly got up. If I am six or seven in 1937, then my father was around forty-three years old. He slowly gets up from his knees, beside my bed, sits down on my bed again, and says, "Sit here, my son."

And then he said—and I will never forget this!—

[By now Dr. Panosian is in tears, and I dare not speak.]

He said, "Now, Edvert, I want you to know that what you just did to me did not hurt me *half* as much as how you hurt me when I heard what you have done."

And then he stopped, and he said, "Don't *ever* steal again."

That's all. We went downstairs, and nothing more was ever said about it. But for eighty years, I've not been able to steal. [Here Panosian laughs, but it's the kind of laughter that erupts from someone amidst tears. I finally breathed.]

That's the only discipline I remember—but I *remember* it. What wisdom! What sensitivity! That has stuck with me. I can feel it yet: I'm striking my father, which is against all comprehension. I can't *do* this, and yet I'm *ordered* to do it! And I can hear him say, "Harder!" Talk about psychology! Talk about education! Profound.

Think of how our Heavenly Father grieves over His children.

That moment has stuck with Dr. Panosian throughout his entire life. And after hearing him relive it so poignantly, it will stick with me as well.

Panosian family, circa 1937; back row, left to right: the wife of Mihran Momjian (Ed's aunt),
Emma Momjian (Ed's grandmother), Manny Panosian (Ed's brother), Sara Panosian
(Ed's mother), Jimmy Panosian (Ed's brother), and partially including Nazar Panosian
(Ed's father); front row, left to right: Eddie Panosian, Ronnie Momjian
(Ed's cousin and Mihran's son), and Ruth Panosian (Ed's sister)

In part because of the impression made on him by his father's masterful lesson, Ed Panosian was not a difficult child. He was obedient and conscientious. In fact, he recalls being teased by his siblings for being such "a good boy." He had sowed his wild oats at age seven.

Ed Panosian was also a good student. Usually. He tells of one class where his performance was subpar. It was a history class, of all things, and the shrewd teacher changed his life:

> I had a junior high history teacher. She was an outstanding teacher—Miss McGinnus was her name. She could have been a college teacher. I don't know if she had a Ph.D., but she was excellent. She sensed that I was coasting in her class; so at some marking period, at five weeks or whatever they had, she gave me an "F" in the course. I had earned it, but I never expected to get it because my name was Panosian, and there had been three scholars [siblings] before me. I was incensed at her betrayal, and I decided—which was exactly what she intended—"I'll show her!" And I began to study, and then I began to like history as a result.

Our conversations about Dr. Panosian's boyhood often turned to his father. Nazar Panosian was a proud and devoted American—which is not to say he was without opinions as to how his new country should be run. Dr. Panosian explains:

> I remember a great deal of listening to the radio at my father's insistence. We listened every evening to Lowell Thomas, Fulton Lewis Jr., H. V. Kaltenborn.[129] They were standard fare; and the most important piece of furniture in our living room was a console model walnut Sears Silvertone radio. We listened to that, and my dad made comments along the way, expressing his opinions about political actions: *"That's no way to run a country!"* and this kind of thing. We used to humorously regret that there wasn't a direct line from our living room to the Oval Office so that they could get the benefit of my dad's wisdom. But every time it was over, Dad would say, "But children, remember, this is the best country there is!" He would be openly critical, but he always made sure we knew how blessed we were to live in America.

---

[129] Thomas, Lewis, and Kaltenborn were conservative American radio commentators from the 1930s through the 1960s.

I asked about Dr. Panosian's other interests as a young man. Music? Not really, though he played violin and viola in high school, before the superior musicians at BJU convinced him to retire from his short-lived strings career. Sports? Certainly not. He explained:

> I didn't have the *time* for sports. Manny had gone off to fight the war [World War II], and we had to keep the home front—we had to keep the store going. Dad had employees, but I would go and do things like unpacking cartons and shipments of shoes, putting them on the shelf, and so forth. Eventually I got on the fitting floor and sold shoes. I fit children. The business was built on *fitting*. Today nobody wants fitting; they just want price. We carried quality merchandise, and we fit the customer. For children, that's very important.

Ed Panosian chose not to invest his adult life in the shoe business, but he certainly learned the store's talking points from his father. The memory of "fitting" causes him to launch into another story in which his father is the hero:

> Dad, when he was still shoemaking and repairing, would regularly have customers come in with a prescription, written by a doctor, addressed to Mr. Panosian—not to anybody in general, but to *Mr. Panosian*—to modify a shoe. A quarter-inch lift on this side, or a one-inch cork platform for a child with one leg shorter than the other. He would add the platform and cover it with the same leather that was on the other shoe, and it was hardly visible. Dad was so proud! Here is a third-grade-educated cobbler, getting a prescription from a *medical doctor,* addressed to *him*—to do what nobody else in town can do! [Panosian is shouting by now, theatrically, for an audience of one.] My father would never have boasted like that, of course. But that was the honor he felt.

Recalling that a question about sports had provoked those memories, he returned to the topic by telling of a few times when his grandchildren have been listed in the newspaper for some awards won during a season of sports, "usually in the fine print." He reveled at the accomplishment: "That's the first time a *Panosian* has been on the sports page in history!" As I had come to expect, this self-inflicted barb elicited a great laugh from its speaker.

———————

Although Edward was a good boy, he wasn't yet a Christian. He knows now that goodness—a supposed self-made righteousness—can be damning. But he didn't yet know this during his teenage years.

In God's providence, Panosian went away to a Christian summer camp when he was fifteen years old. There, for the first time in his life, he understood that he was hopelessly lost in sin.[130] He understood that he could do nothing to save himself, and that he needed a Savior.[131] He understood that Jesus *is* that Savior—"the way, the truth, and the life"—the only way to have peace with God.[132] He learned that Jesus had died as his substitute, taking the punishment which his sins deserved[133]—much as his father had done when he was a seven-year-old thief. He understood the gospel, and he believed it.

Days before his fifteenth birthday, on August 15, 1945, Ed Panosian was born again through faith in Jesus Christ.

---

[130] Romans 3:10–11, 23; Romans 6:23.
[131] Ephesians 2:8–9.
[132] John 14:6 KJV.
[133] 1 Peter 3:18.

CHAPTER NINETEEN

THE STORY GIRL

1947–1950 — CONNELLSVILLE, PENNSYLVANIA
AND GREENVILLE, SOUTH CAROLINA

"The beauty of winter is that it makes you appreciate spring."

—L. M. Montgomery[134]

Betty Snyder was born in Vanderbilt, Pennsylvania, a suburb of Pittsburgh, to George and Mary Snyder. She was the eldest of four children—two girls and two boys. Her childhood wasn't without its joys, but neither was it without its sorrows. By the time Betty was a teenager, she and her siblings were being raised solely by their mother. "My mother was divorced. My father was an alcoholic. That's one of the reasons why I never wanted to get married. I could see what a marriage could be."

Mrs. Panosian recalls the fear she felt when her father would pick her up from an event in his car. She knew that the drive would often be harrowing as a result of his incessant drinking. "My father's sister—my aunt—said that a neighbor taught my father to drink. Social drinkers do not know the heartache and devastation they bring." But Betty and her family certainly knew, and she was determined that alcohol would never have a place in her life.

Thankfully, Betty's mother withstood the loss of her husband and had the resilience and resourcefulness to raise four children on her own. Being a single mother is difficult now, and it was even more dif-

---

[134] Lucy Maud Montgomery, *The Story Girl* (Boston: L. C. Page, 1911), 21.

ficult in the 1930s and 1940s. Yet, Betty looks back on her childhood with a deep admiration for her mother. "My mother was a very kind, courageous woman."

From a young age, Betty enjoyed telling stories. She was a fearless performer. "I always loved stories as I was growing up," she explains. "In fact, even when I was in grade school, the teacher would ask me, 'Could you tell us what happened in the assignment for today?' And I would stand up and tell them! I've always had a strong voice. I can remember they always called on me to read the Bible at the beginning of classes in public school. Those were the days when they did read the Bible, and prayed, before beginning class."

The Snyder children attended a church, but not one that preached the gospel. Betty's exposure to the Bible was basically limited to her morning readings with her classmates. However, in yet another display of God's gracious providence, she formed a friendship with a Christian:

> When I attended Dunbar Township High School in Connellsville, I met the girl who became my best friend—Cecelia Richter (now Mrs. James Meena). Her family knew the Lord, and her sisters attended Moody Bible Institute in Chicago. One summer, Cecelia and I went to Chicago to visit them. I thought that was a big deal, because we'd go on a train alone to Chicago, and it was just something wonderful! We had a good time visiting and seeing all the sights of Chicago.

> Youth for Christ had a Saturday evening cruise, a moonlight cruise, on Lake Michigan—an evangelistic event. The preacher was such a wonderful preacher, such a biblical preacher, and rather charismatic. It was there that I accepted the Lord as my Savior.

> When we returned home, we had Bible school, and we attended regular Youth for Christ meetings. I met a blessed lady named Mary Parkhill, a second-grade teacher, who gathered young Christians in her home and really helped us grow in the Lord.

Cecilia was instrumental in bringing Betty to Christ. She would also be used of the Lord to lead Betty to Bob Jones University far away in South Carolina. Little did Betty know that she would remain at that educational institution for over seventy years. "When Cecilia decided to attend Bob Jones University, I felt that was the place for me, too." Betty enrolled as a freshman in 1947—the school's first year in Greenville, South Carolina, and the first year "Bob Jones College" became "Bob Jones University." The campus is beautiful now—it was not then. Betty explains, "It was the loneliest, most barren campus—hardly a tree, hardly a sidewalk. . . . And I remember seeing all this red mud. I had never seen so much mud!" Yet, she was thrilled to be there. She was only sixteen years old when she moved away to college—a testament to her desire to escape the hardships of her childhood as much as to her academic abilities. Dr. Panosian shares, "Her first night in the dormitory was one of relief—of peace."

To help pay for Betty's college education, her mother took as many hours as she could get at Connellsville's Anchor Hocking factory, making glass bottles and kitchen containers. Betty waited tables at the university and worked summers at Anchor Hocking to help pay for her schooling. She considered going into nursing, but she opted instead to major in speech—a decision that uniquely prepared her for her life's work and ministry.[135]

During Betty's junior year, she was given the opportunity to do live radio for the university's fledgling radio station, WMUU. The station was started by BJU in 1947, and it served as an ancillary ministry of the school until it was sold in 2012. Early programming included preaching, music, and daily serial radio programs. Betty was invited to perform in the daily dramas. Since the programs aired live, the pressure on the students was immense—a memorable, often comical experience. Even now, Betty laughs to recall a young man's efforts to stifle a sneeze while on the air. "He was going into all kinds of contortions to stop it, because it would just *ruin* the whole thing—'on air.' He finally put his head under the cushions of the sofa!" One particular member of the audience contributed to the students' stress. Dr. Bob Jones Jr., accomplished actor, public speaker, and BJU's president at the time, was home ill, so he would often tune in to broadcasts. Any time there were mistakes—poor diction, an unnecessary noise, or a

[135] Years later, Betty fainted during the blood test required to obtain her marriage license, comically verifying that her decision to pass on the medical field had been a wise one.

mispronounced word in the newscast—he would call in and tell them to "shape up!"

Ironically, the radio dramas served as a sort of "matchmaker" for Betty. In order to participate in the productions, she was permitted to leave her eighth-period history class early. She needed a fellow student—preferably someone proficient in history—to teach her what she had missed each of those class days. And in God's providence, she chose a lanky, good-natured sophomore from the state of New York. The young man's name was Ed, and he was happy to oblige.

CHAPTER TWENTY

A RELUCTANT ROMANCE

1948 — ELMIRA, NEW YORK
AND GREENVILLE, SOUTH CAROLINA

"This is a way to kill a wife with kindness,
And thus I'll curb her mad and headstrong humour.
He that knows better how to tame a shrew,
Now let him speak. 'Tis charity to show."

—William Shakespeare[136]

Ed Panosian was a senior in high school, just a few months away from graduation. He was uncertain what he wanted to do with his life. He did know one thing, however: he didn't want to work in the family shoe business. God had blessed his parents with a thriving company, Panosian's Shoes. His father, Nazar, had done extremely well for himself, despite his third-grade education. Ed, like his siblings, had worked in the store after school and in the summers, and he was glad to do so. He learned the value of hard work. But he also learned that selling shoes wasn't what he wanted to do with the rest of his life. His older brother Manny was in line to take over the family business, and that was perfectly fine with Ed.

Ed hoped to go to college, though he didn't know where nor what he would study. God providentially worked out his education, albeit in an unexpected way. Ed Panosian was introduced to Bob Jones University through an advertisement on the back of *The Etude*, a piano

---

[136] Barbara Mowat, Paul Werstine, Michael Poston, Rebecca Niles, eds., *The Taming of the Shrew* (Washington: Folger Shakespeare Library, n.d.), accessed August 27, 2018. www.folger-digitaltexts.org.

magazine. That might not seem unusual. But Ed didn't play the piano. He did play a bit of tennis. His partner on the court, Doris Everett, taught child evangelism courses with a piano teacher friend who saw those back-cover ads for Bob Jones College. When Doris was looking for a college, the teacher—a Miss Beidelman, who, according to Dr. Panosian, "had apparently been bombarded for years with this ad, and had heard of Bob Jones the evangelist"—recommended the school. When it was Ed's turn to look for a college, Doris' experience at BJU encouraged him to attend as well. And so he did.

God is sovereign: "Our God is in the heavens: he hath done whatsoever he hath pleased."[137] And occasionally He does what He pleases in ways so brilliantly tortuous that there is no possible explanation but Him. Ed Panosian—the iconic professor without whom whole decades of life at BJU would be almost unrecognizable—might never have heard about the school apart from an unlikely series of coincidences. Better, *providences.*

Ed—or Eddie, to be precise—enrolled at BJU with a Bible major and a history minor. He loved being in college, and he loved being out of his siblings' shadows:

> For the first time, I was here on my own. There was no reputation to precede me, and it was good for me to get away from home and where I was not known. For the first time, also, I insisted on abandoning what my classmates and family had called me, because I was "Eddie" at home, and I never liked it. Now I could be "Ed," because I was starting afresh, and I liked that better.

God worked in Ed Panosian's life through the preaching of the Word almost immediately upon his arrival on campus. He recalls a specific message by Dr. Bob Jones Sr. that altered his life:

> I remember one of the first opening evangelistic services that the founder preached, and when he looked us in the eyes and said, "No man having put his hand to the plow and looking back is *fit* for the kingdom of God."[138] Well, he stopped right there—"is *fit,*" period.

---

[137] Psalm 115:3 KJV.
[138] Luke 9:62 KJV.

And he spoke to homesick freshmen and raked us over the coals: "That's the only problem with you—you're just not *fit!*" And I remember my path to ministry and service began that night.

———————

Ed Panosian and Betty Snyder first met in the classroom, during his first year at BJU. Dr. Panosian tells of their meeting—and of their mischievous misconduct in a class he considered less-than-stellar:

> There was a course—the only education course I ever had—which was Educational Psychology. I remember being bored at the theoretical nature of the content. I came in the first day and asked Betty Snyder if the seat next to her was taken. She said, "No, sit down, come on." And that began a relationship; and I confess that we played tic-tac-toe in that class to pass the time. [This last confession is spoken through a bit of embarrassed laughter.]

Fast forward to Ed's sophomore year. One of his history classes met during eighth period, right at the end of the day. The class wasn't large; none were, as there were no large lecture classes at BJU at the time. When Betty needed some tutoring because she had to leave class early to perform on a live radio program, Ed was happy to help. She explains how her tic-tac-toe partner became her tutor: "I looked around the class to see who made the As, and I saw Ed. He always knew everything. And so I asked him if he'd help me; and he's been helping me ever since."

Asked if she had ulterior motives in asking for Ed's help—if she "had her eye on him"—Betty gave this firm response, through a giggle: "No, no, no! I had my eye on passing!"

Ed and Betty were friends and study partners. That was it. Looking back, they explain it, together, finishing each other's sentences: "There was no immediate attraction. It was gradual. We both needed to be convinced a little bit."

For one thing, Betty was still skeptical about romance in general. And if she *had* been looking for romance—well, in 1950 BJU was crawling with GI's who were returning from the war. "They had purpose. Some of them were older than their GA faculty members. They were really quite remarkable—very focused and determined," Betty says. Ed readily agrees, adding, "And they were accustomed to discipline." Ed and Betty were part of the Greatest Generation. They had goals, and those goals wouldn't be denied for a relationship.

In time, however, both did become increasingly convinced. In need of a date to accompany him on his society's outing, Ed recalled how much he had enjoyed Betty's company during their tutoring sessions. They attended the event together, their first real "date." Friendship grew into courtship. Courtship eventually led to a proposal: Ed asked Betty to marry him during the annual campus Bible Conference in 1952, and she said *yes*. Kind of.

"When I asked her to marry me," Ed explains, "she said, 'Yes, but I don't know when.' It took a while for her to get acclimated to the idea. Her experience observing her parents' marriage was not healthy." Betty recalls her answer as sensible, aided by an ironic grin, "I gave him time to decide if he really *wanted* to marry me."

Betty graduated with a bachelor of arts in speech in 1951, a year ahead of Ed. She stayed at BJU as a graduate assistant, teaching Freshman Speech while she earned a master of arts in speech. Upon his graduation in 1952, Ed accepted a graduate assistantship, too. Of course, Betty was still a year ahead, finishing her second degree in 1953. While Ed completed his master's degree, and while they contemplated marriage, Betty moved back home to Connellsville, Pennsylvania, and accepted a position teaching sixth grade at a local public school for a year. Her salary for that year was $2,400.

Ed finished his master of arts degree in church history in 1954, and Betty could delay no longer. Reluctant as she may have been since childhood, she had fallen in love, and with a man very unlike her father. Ed and Betty wed on June 12, 1954. Unlike most of the Panosian wives, Betty was *not* an Armenian. Ed's mother, Sara Momjian Panosian—who had been through so much in Turkey before immigrating to the United States—proudly and perpetually introduced her daughter-in-law to her Armenian friends as "the American."

If the Panosians' romance took some time to kindle, it has certainly burned long and bright. Dr. Panosian, in a 1999 interview with *The Collegian* (the BJU student paper), described his deep affection for his wife: "I used to think I could eat her up, I was so in love with her. But we have come to love each other far more."[139]

Ed and Betty's wedding: June 12, 1954

---

[139] Elena Hines, "Faculty Love Stories Fill Hearts," *The Collegian* (Greenville, SC), Feb. 4, 1999.

Betty embarking on her honeymoon, 1954

Following a honeymoon in New Hampshire, the Panosians returned to Greenville, where they both joined the faculty of Bob Jones University. They were part of a group of young people who would become pillars of the institution, including Richard and Betty Rupp, Gene and Lucille Fisher, Dwight and Gwen Gustafson, Gail and Alice Gingery, and Joe and Grace Henson, among others.

For her part, Betty would teach speech for forty-eight years at BJU, especially focusing on courses such as Freshman Speech and Storytelling, and private lessons.

She would also become a regular on the stage of Rodeheaver Auditorium at BJU, performing in and directing Sunday fine arts "vespers" programs and acting in multiple Shakespearean plays. Each time she performed felt a bit like torture for Betty. She would become terrified as she waited in the green room or in the wings: "Before I went on stage, I always wondered, 'Why did you get into this?' We had no prompters, and in those days we had to make ourselves heard without any amplification." If she was nervous, the audience couldn't tell as they watched her play the rebellious Kate to Ed's relentless Petruchio in *The Taming of the Shrew*, which—to the delight of audiences—they performed together three times, in 1961, 1971, and 1981. An article from *The Greenville News*, dated May 28, 1971, hails them both:

> A turn-away audience . . . was kept in roars of laughter by the lusty, brawling, bickering comedy. Starring was Edward Panosian as Petruchio who tamed his lovely shrew, Katherine, a role filled most capably by his wife, Betty. . . . The Panosians, admirably suited in every way to their roles, proved perfect foils for each other. Buffeted and buffeting, wrangling and jangling, little by little Petruchio tames his Kate until when he commands, "Kiss me, Kate," she does so with considerable willingness.[140]

By the time the Panosians performed in that 1971 production, they had three children. The children's reaction to their parents' performances was less enthusiastic than the newspaper's review. Colleague

---

[140] Lucille B. Green, "'Taming of Shrew' Called Lusty Comedy," *Greenville News* (Greenville, SC), May 28, 1971.

Linda Hayner explains in an excerpt from her speech on the occasion of Dr. Panosian's retirement banquet: "Dr. and Mrs. Panosian rehearsed their [*Taming of the Shrew*] lines at home until they discovered that their children thought they were truly fighting. Rehearsals were moved outside the home."

Betty Panosian eventually took her acting abilities from the stage to the screen, playing alongside Ed once again in the University's full-length film drama *The Printing*.

Perhaps most enjoyably of all, she regularly returned to her first love of storytelling. Betty became a fixture at WMUU, hosting her own serial radio program for twenty years: "Stories for Kids with Betty Panosian." Every Friday evening, she would charm audiences by reading classic children's literature. Outside of the studio, she taught missionary stories in countless vacation Bible schools. And perhaps most telling of all, she took special pleasure in reading stories to young patients at the local Shriners Children's Hospital, often with her daughter Lisa coming along as her storytelling partner.

Betty's stories have ridden the airwaves to thousands of children, bringing Christian classics like *The Pilgrim's Progress* to life with her unique delivery that is somehow both captivating and soothing. Only eternity will reveal how far those stories have gone. But occasionally we get a glimpse. A missionary recently called Betty. She told her that she had been in Chile, and in the most unexpected place, she heard Betty's voice. Years before, another missionary had recorded Betty's stories and taken them to the mission field with her as a piece of home—a gift to herself and her children.

Some eighty years later, the young story girl from Connellsville continues to tell stories.

In Shakespeare's *The Taming of the Shrew,* the willful Kate vows never to marry. Betty was never a shrew, nor did she need taming. But, like the character she portrayed thrice on the stage of Rodeheaver Auditorium, she had resolved never to wed. Thankfully, life imitated art, and in God's ironic providence, a Petruchio named Panosian changed her mind.

CHAPTER TWENTY—ONE

THE ICONIC PROFESSOR

1952–2004 — GREENVILLE, SOUTH CAROLINA

*"Our hearers inevitably are drawn to that about which we are
most passionate. Every teacher knows that. My students are
unlikely to learn all that I teach them. I've resigned myself to that
for a long time. They're most likely to learn what I'm excited about."*

—D. A. Carson[141]

*"The lectern has been my pulpit for fifty years,
and I thank God for that."*

—Edward M. Panosian

Ed Panosian started teaching at Bob Jones University in 1952, as a graduate assistant. His formal teaching ministry at the university continued for fifty-two years until he retired in 2004 at the age of seventy-three. No teacher in the history of BJU has taught more students—an estimated thirty thousand young people. Panosian has been used of the Lord as a writer, lecturer, and actor. But he is first and foremost a teacher.

As a graduate assistant during the 1952 and 1953 school years, Panosian taught several sections of History of Civ. There were no large lecture classes at the time, so freshmen learned history in several classes of thirty to forty students each. One of several different instructors taught each class.

---

[141] D. A. Carson, "What Is the Gospel?" (Sermon, The Gospel Coalition Conference, Trinity Evangelical Divinity School, Deerfield, IL, May 28, 2007).

When his grad assistantship concluded in 1954, Panosian was one
of those offered a job as a full-time faculty member. He was especially
noted by the Dean of the School of Religion, Dr. Charles Brokenshire. Brokenshire—now known primarily for the men's dormitory
that bears his name—was an unsurpassed scholar, both in linguistics
and theology. He had been trained in the orthodox tradition of the old
Princeton Seminary, under such theological giants as B. B. Warfield
and J. Gresham Machen. Upon his arrival at BJU in 1943, Brokenshire
brought an unmistakable commitment to scholarship to the university.
BJU was founded through the fire of revivalist preaching by men like
Dr. Bob Jones Sr. But it grew into an elite academic institution and
fortress of the faith through the light of true Christian scholarship by
men like Charles Brokenshire. Campus historian Dan Turner gives a
sample of the Brokenshire intellect:

> His faculty record [he taught first at Alma College in Michigan]
> from 1930 stated that he had "a reading knowledge or better" of
> French, Portuguese, German, Dutch, Spanish, Italian, Swedish,
> Norse, Latin, Greek (both classical and Koine), Hebrew, "Chaldee"
> (biblical Aramaic), modern Greek, Yiddish, Arabic, Syriac, Samari-
> tan, Ethiopic, Babylonian, Coptic, Egyptian Hieroglyph, and Espe-
> ranto. By the end of his teaching career, he had added Chinese, Japa-
> nese, and Russian to the list.[142]

Brokenshire took an interest in young Ed Panosian, who had
earned his bachelor's degree in Bible and was almost finished with
his master's degree in church history. It was the latter that intrigued
Dr. Brokenshire. The church history program was fairly new, so the
instruction was very personal. The two of them read Philip Schaff's
eight-volume *History of the Christian Church* together—one volume
every two weeks—then met to discuss it. Panosian explains:

> We met in my office in the old Alumni Faculty Wing, number four-
> teen, I think it was, or sixteen. He would sit in an armchair and lean
> back, and he would ask me questions; and I would answer them.
> Then he would tell me what else I should know and give me assign-

---

[142] Daniel L. Turner, *Standing without Apology: The History of Bob Jones University* (Greenville, SC: BJU Press, 2001), 278.

ments. We met once a week, and so forth. That was a dear opportunity, a cherished experience.

Brokenshire devised a plan through which Panosian would begin his doctoral studies in church history, while also starting to teach church history classes in the university. He planned for Panosian to take doctoral-level classes at respected (albeit liberal) institutions around the country in addition to his normal doctoral coursework at BJU. Brokenshire warned him that the theology at the respected schools was heresy, but he encouraged him to take advantage of their extensive libraries: "You are going there not for what they will teach you—you are going there for their resources. Read their libraries!"

In addition to marrying Betty in the summer of 1954, Ed enrolled in summer classes at Union Seminary in New York City. For the next several years, he studied during the summers with esteemed church history scholars at Fuller Seminary, Garrett Seminary, Tulane University, Columbia University, and the University of Chicago Divinity School. He learned a great deal of history, and he learned to loathe liberal theology. On one occasion, when fundamental doctrines of the faith were being denied in his summer studies, Panosian turned to a classmate, punched his arm, and asked incredulously, "Do you really *believe* this?" His classmate looked back and answered, "Well, some of it."

The exposure to liberal thought was instructive to Dr. Panosian. But at times it was also uncomfortable. He tells of one rather tense interaction with Dr. Robert Handy, who taught American church history at Union:

> Handy, in the class on American Revival History, said—I can hear this yet—"The problem with the American revivalist movement was that it divided all of the population into two groups, saved and unsaved." I spoke up in class and asked, "What others are there?" He spoke to the rest of the class: "Here in our midst is a live example of one of these birds."

Panosian's firsthand experience of theological modernism was an effective inoculation, making him more resistant to it and more committed to the Scriptures than ever. He notes that it also enabled him "to warn generations of graduate students against those infidel scholars and their insidious teachings."

Dr. Brokenshire intended to pass the BJU church history baton on to his promising pupil. He saw the plan's commencement, but he wouldn't see its completion. He died at the end of the 1953–1954 school year at the age of sixty-nine, shortly after his endorsement of Panosian and just days before Panosian's master's degree graduation. BJU lost an anchor of its faculty, but in God's providence, another was being forged. Panosian was asked to fill in as a church history professor—a "temporary" position he held for five decades.

Panosian didn't share Brokenshire's genius for language. But he did share his commitment to the Scriptures. And it will make BJU alumni smile to learn that Dr. Brokenshire was especially known by students in the 1940s and 1950s for his "eccentric" mode of transportation—riding his bicycle around campus. The baton had indeed been passed.[143]

Panosian finished his doctorate in 1959, earning his degree in church history from BJU. In an article on September 1, 1959, *The Greenville Piedmont* hailed the accomplishment:

> Dr. Panosian's degree was granted in the field of church history. His dissertation was written on the subject, "An Historical Investigation of Luther's Doctrine of Scriptural Authority with Critical Evaluation of Representative Contemporary Interpretations." . . . In preparing his dissertation, Dr. Panosian did extensive research in libraries throughout the eastern section of the country and several other colleges and universities, including Columbia University, Garrett Biblical Institute at Evanston, Ill. and the University of Chicago.[144]

Martin Luther continues to be Panosian's favorite character from church history.

---

[143] In an interview with John Matzko, Betty Panosian shared her comical impression of Dr. Brokenshire: "I just always remember seeing him riding his bike with ribbons on his bike and his pockets full of books. And I often thought he really needed a wife to press his clothes!"

[144] "Doctorates Conferred on BJU Faculty Pair." *Greenville Piedmont,* (Greenville, SC), Sept. 1, 1959.

In addition to his own teaching responsibilities, Dr. Panosian received educational honors and held leadership positions among his peers. In 1952 he was elected president of his undergrad senior class. In 1960 he was elected to membership in the American Society of Church History.[145] The same year he was made the chairman of the Division of Social Science in the College of Arts and Science, a role he continued to fill until 2000. In 1970 and 1972 he was chosen as an "Outstanding Educator of America" based on his civic and professional achievements.[146] He was listed in *Who's Who Among Educators in America*.[147] He was twice elected president of the BJU Alumni Association, besides serving in multiple other offices. In 1983 *The Vintage* (the yearbook of BJU) was dedicated to him.[148] The dedicatory page called him "one of the University's finest educators" and described his influence on his students:

> To a generation of graduates, the mention of his name brings to mind not only his deep, resonant voice filling his classroom but also his godly and consistent example of Christian service.[149]

In 1984 Dr. Panosian was honored with the Alumni Association's Alumni Appreciation Award "in recognition of outstanding Christian leadership and service to young lives through the ministry of Bob Jones University."[150]

During his teaching career, Dr. Panosian taught and designed the following courses: Reformation, Renaissance, Ancient and Medieval Philosophy, Rome, American History, British Empire and Imperialism, Philosophy of History, and Historical Liberalism.

Having described the classes he taught, the positions he held, and the fifty-two-year duration of his teaching ministry, Panosian concluded with a comedic sigh: "Wow. That all tires me out just recounting it!" Indeed.

---

[145] *Faculty Notes* 2, no. 5 (1960): 2.

[146] "Outstanding Educators of America," *Voice of the Alumni* 44, no. 4 (Dec. 1970): 7. "BJU Faculty Are Chosen," *Voice of the Alumni* 46, no. 1 (June 1972): 2.

[147] Bob Jones University, *Vintage* (Greenville, SC: 1983), 14 , BJU Archives.

[148] "Yearbooks Dedicated." *Faith for the Family* 11, no. 6 (July/August 1983): 18.

[149] *Vintage,* 1983, 14.

[150] "Alumni Appreciation Award." *Faith for the Family* 12, no. 2, (Feb. 1984): 16.

Although Dr. Panosian taught a wide variety of courses, History of Civ was the one for which he was famous. It was a notoriously challenging class—a "rite of passage" for BJU students, most of whom took it as freshmen. *Survive History of Civ and you're going to survive college*—that was the mindset. It was an almost impossibly ambitious course in its scope, essentially covering the history of every people in every age in every part of the world. "The History of Everything." Proportional to the size of the syllabus was the size of the classes. From the mid-1960s, Dr. Panosian taught History of Civ to roughly one thousand students per year, divided into only two or three class periods.[151] Every Monday and Wednesday he would enter the Concert Center (now called Stratton Hall) to face hundreds of eighteen- and nineteen-year-olds, armed only with an overhead projector, a lectern, and his own passion to display the hand of God in human history.

Ed in the History Department Office, 1972; photo courtesy of Bob Jones University

---

[151] Dr. Panosian explains that the concept of dividing a three-hour college course into two hours of lecture by a single professor, complemented by an hour of discussion in small classes, was an innovation of Woodrow Wilson's during his presidency at Princeton University. It was intended to standardize the lectures while also allowing for discussion and reinforcement in small groups of ten to twenty students per instructor.

Asked to share his approach to History of Civ, Panosian penned the following answer:

> I was concerned, in teaching history to young people, to help them see the Hand of God in the affairs of men all through the past, that they might grow to see that the same Hand does—and will—guide and govern the one who is yielded to do His will. I wanted students to know that, while man *thinks* he is "running things" in this world, God is working out His purposes, for His glory and for man's ultimate good. While dates, events, and personnel are all important components of man's history over the centuries, this underlying principle is what has motivated my labor. I trust that with some it has succeeded, to His glory.

Indeed, it has. Those who have sat under Dr. Panosian's ministry have been altered by it. For some (myself included), he "rescued" history from the slander that it is tedious and boring. He demonstrated that history—rightly understood, which means rightly *taught*—is thrilling. One of his students, Alfonso Cavazos, comments, "I loved how dramatic his lectures were. He made history come alive." Susanne Anderson, another of his students, concurs, speaking for countless others:

> History was a dry subject to me after my high school experience. Dr. Panosian awakened in me an appreciation for History of Civ when he described the everyday life of a Roman soldier. Suddenly, history was about *people* and not just dates on a calendar.

For my part, I have often mused that Panosian's genius was "wasted on freshmen." It may be true that I would have learned more if I had taken the course as an upperclassman. I certainly learned more as a graduate student in Church History. But those two semesters of my freshman year were no waste. Dr. Panosian taught thousands of eighteen-year-olds to enjoy learning, to work hard, and to be incurably curious.

The only thing better than hearing Dr. Panosian teach church history from a lectern or pulpit would have been hearing his lectures on the very sites where the events he described took place. Over the span of thirty-six years, between 1969 and 2005, that was possible, as Dr. Panosian led a total of thirteen study tours to Reformation sites. On various trips, Dr. Panosian lectured in Italy, Switzerland, Germany, France, Austria, Belgium, and England. A typical trip included twenty to forty people and lasted three weeks. Panosian shares his mother's response when he informed her that he would be leading tours to Europe:

> I remember in 1969 when I first announced by phone that this opportunity was being contemplated. My mother's reaction was "Edvert, why do you want to go there? Everything is *old!*" As a history teacher, that was exactly why I wanted to go! My parents had no desire ever to visit "the old country." It represented to them pain and heartache.

Those who were fortunate enough to accompany Dr. Panosian on the trips considered them once-in-a-lifetime opportunities. Retired BJU staff member Gail Yost describes her experience from 2003, which took her to Rome, Florence, Milan, Geneva, Constance, Worms, Rothenburg, Luxembourg, Paris, and London:

> In every city, a local guide led us through the sites and explained their significance. Then, in half-hour evening meetings back at the hotel, Dr. Panosian would flesh out what we had seen and heard, helping us connect it to the Reformation and its expansion throughout Europe.[152]

Of course, new history is unfolding every day. It happened, in unforgettable ways, during Panosian's tenure at BJU. Presidents came and went. Wars were waged. Society changed. Panosian taught history during the last half of the twentieth century—a time when the world changed more significantly and rapidly than at any other time in "the history of civilization." BJU alumnus Nick Griffin offers a poignant example, recalling a tragic time in our nation's history: "I remember going to History of Civ right after President Kennedy's assassination. What a comfort Dr. Panosian was to all in that class that afternoon." Panosian would shepherd his students through the Vietnam War, Watergate, and the end of the Cold War. Marsha Landry, another graduate, remembers:

---

[152] Gail Yost, "An Experience of a Lifetime," *Voice of the Alumni* 76, no. 5, (2003): 14.

I recall a History of Civ class on Friday, November 10, 1989. I can hear him still. I don't remember the exact words, but it was something to this effect: "Yesterday will go down in history. Yesterday the Wall came down." He then went on to explain the significance of that great event. I recall there being a lot of celebrating, clapping, and cheering.

Dr. Panosian uttered millions of words during his fifty-two years of history lectures. Many of them are permanently etched into the memories of his students. I offer a few, with thanks to those who jogged my memory with their own suggestions:

- "History is HIS story."
- "The Holy Roman Empire . . . was neither Holy, nor Roman, nor an Empire."[153]
- "All roads lead to Rome. ALL roads lead to Rome. All ROADS lead to Rome. All roads LEAD to Rome. All roads lead TO Rome. All roads lead to ROME."
- "This, too, shall pass."
- "To err is human; to 'air' is to mispronounce the word."
- "Rococo" (almost whispered, to personify its light, wistful style). "Baroque" (almost shouted, to personify its heavy, serious style).
- "You'll have to use the BACH door because the front door is BAROQUE-in."
- "Take out a half sheet of paper, please." "Did you complete the assigned reading?" And, "EEEEEE!"
- "Participate constructively. Get involved. Have an influence."
- "Among other things, church history teaches us human weakness. All of us are able to commit the worst sin under the right provocation. Conversely, all of us are able to be as faithful as the most faithful given our circumstances."
- "In the history of doctrine, truth is assumed until it is challenged."

---

[153] This statement is credited to Napoleon Bonaparte.

- "In the Middle Ages, people ate what was in season all season long and without seasoning."
- "The theology of the Medieval Church was essentially what the Bible-believer believes, to which tradition—that is, human error—was added. The Bible is our sole and sufficient authority for faith and practice."
- "Truth mixed with error is the most dangerous form of error."
- "I sleep well at night knowing that no one in the world can draw a breath without the permission of an almighty God."
- "That God chooses to redeem *any* is of His unfathomable grace; that He doesn't redeem all is not unfair. None of us wants fairness! None wants what he deserves—hell."
- "The difference between Christianity and every other religion is this: every other religion says, 'Do this and you shall live.' Christianity says, 'Live, and as a result, do this.'"
- "God is great. God is good. And Thou God seest me."
- "God uses human agency to accomplish divine purpose. He Who could command angels to do His bidding, invites men."
- "Two guiding life principles: God is sovereign; I am His servant."

Dr. Panosian—through deep, well prepared lectures, not just sound bites—left lasting impressions on his students. But he made even deeper marks on his fellow teachers, and history teachers were especially shaped by his influence. One, Dr. David Fisher, regards him as a second father.[154] Another, Dr. Brenda Schoolfield, speaks for countless others when she regards him as a mentor and example:

> From the time I was a GA in the History Department and through every semester that I taught discussion classes in the Civ program, when I took attendance for a section of lecture, I stayed the whole time to listen. I hear him often in my head while I'm teaching. (I've told him this, and he always apologizes. I assure him of my gratitude.) I observed him deal with the challenges of managing a large

---

[154] See Dr. David Fisher's tribute in the Appendix.

classroom—the sleepers, the homework-doers, the letter-writers. He once advised me "to err on the side of grace." I have found that guidance a kind of guardrail. He was firm with students, but I hope they always knew how much he cared about them.

Yes, students learned not to multi-task in Dr. Panosian's classes. One student's humiliation at being called out for sleeping or studying another subject during Panosian's lectures usually sufficed to prevent the rest of the class from crossing the good doctor for the semester. Students knew: you didn't sleep in chapel when one of the Joneses was preaching, and you didn't study outside material in Dr. Panosian's class.

Occasionally, Panosian's correction went unexpectedly sideways. Alumna Jennifer Whitehead recalls such a time:

> In his History of Civ class, my now-husband Dan was whispering with his neighbor, as they wondered what Dr. Panosian's shoe size was. (He had noticeably large feet.) Dr. Panosian called them out for talking: "Excuse me, is there a question?" Dan took a deep breath, then replied: "Umm, well, we, umm, just wondered what size shoe you wear?" Dr. Panosian, apparently amused, replied matter-of-factly: "Size fourteen. Will that be all?"

Not all confrontations ended with a smile. Occasionally, Dr. Panosian would reflect afterward and determine that he had *not* "erred on the side of grace." Those circumstances became lessons in humility, perhaps more significant than the lessons in history. Kim Mowry Melton tells of one such circumstance:

> I remember a class where he called out a student for sleeping and asked to see him after class. The next class, Dr. Panosian humbly apologized to the young man publicly and told us that while the rest of us were sleeping, that student was working security—campus night-watch—keeping us safe.

A similar circumstance demonstrated Panosian's love for his students in an even deeper way. Pastor Paul Whitt relates the story:

> I took History of Civ as a sophomore with a freshman from Oklahoma who was in my prayer group. He came from a very broken home with little financial support—or any other kind of support. Early in the semester, Dr. Panosian stopped mid-lecture and stared at him. "Young man, are my lectures not worthy of your notetaking?" he asked in that booming, echoing voice.

My friend responded, "Excuse me?"

"Why aren't you taking notes?" Dr. Panosian countered.

"Oh, I don't have enough money for a notebook yet. I'm hoping to sell some things this weekend to buy some notebooks and pens," he responded.

"Come see me after class," Dr. Panosian instructed.

I had another class, so I didn't stay to see what happened, but that night in prayer group the freshman shared the results. After class, Dr. Panosian arranged to pick him up that evening. He took him to dinner, then shopping for school supplies and some new clothes. He unofficially adopted him for the rest of the year and made sure he finished the school year.

For me, being a relatively new Christian at the time, it was one of the first examples of discipleship I ever observed.

Dr. Bob Jones III, who served as the president of BJU for many of the years Dr. Panosian taught, offers the following commentary on his teaching ministry:

> During the forty-eight years Dr. Panosian taught History of Civilization to freshman students, his courses, primarily because of his quizzes, were the most feared on campus, but in the aftermath, were the most appreciated. He was beloved by his students because he was a master teacher who greatly loved them, and they knew it.
>
> During my years as BJU president, there was no faculty member that I respected more and depended on more to reflect the values of Christian higher education as represented at BJU. My respect for him is profound. It was a sad day for me and all of his colleagues when he retired. He and his wife together gave a combined one hundred years of sacrificial service here at BJU, the place of their divine appointment.

After forty-eight years, Dr. Panosian finally taught his last History of Civ class in the spring of 2000. It was the end of an era. He handled the closing of the chapter with his typical dignity, charm, and wit. John Mark Steel was taking a church history course with him the very next hour, and he recalls Dr. Panosian's nostalgic comment: "This is the end of the history of civilization as we have known it."

Dr. Panosian continued teaching other courses for four more years before finally retiring from teaching in 2004. He reflects on his last day of classroom instruction:

After that last class, after fifty-two years, I rode my bike to my campus home, as I had done for years before, in my suit and tie, with my briefcase on the rack behind my seat. Just as I turned into my driveway, my rear tire went flat! That had never happened before. It was such a fitting "punctuation mark" on my career. When my friend Dr. Joe Henson heard of the experience, he remarked—in his typical droll manner—"That puts a new meaning on re-tire-ment!"

Dr. Panosian left a profound mark on thousands upon thousands of students during his half-century of instruction. Dr. Charles Barrett, who himself pursued a doctorate in Church History precisely because of Dr. Panosian's influence, is a striking representative of that influence:

> One of the high privileges of my education was to sit under the teaching of Dr. Panosian. His knowledge of church history and his delivery of the same was and continues to be both breathtaking and captivating. His ability to trace historic movements of thought and events to shed light on the present continues to shape my own understanding of church history. He taught his students to discerningly trace God's providence, while being careful not to interpret the reasons behind it. In doing so, we not only learned how to study history, but also how to trust in the all-wise God behind history. There are certainly the memorable quips and eloquent one-liners from class. I recall the repeated quoting of some anonymous citation before every final exam: "Education is what you remember after you have forgotten what you have learned." Sadly, I have forgotten more than I would like to admit from Dr. Panosian. However, more than the lectures, the sense of humor, the eloquence of "the Voice," I remember Dr. Panosian's genuine piety. His love for Christ and his humble, Christ-like life, above all, are to be remembered, commended, and imitated. When I think of Dr. Panosian, and I do so often, I think of how great our Lord and Savior Jesus Christ is. I would guess that is what the good doctor would want.

Reflecting on his teaching ministry, Dr. Panosian states, "The lectern has been my pulpit for fifty years, and I thank God for that." He was the consummate professor, and he taught his students many life-changing lessons. Some of them took place in the classroom. All of them overflowed from his exemplary character and his own walk with God.

CHAPTER TWENTY—TWO

THE INIMITABLE PERFORMER

1952–PRESENT — GREENVILLE, SOUTH CAROLINA
AND AROUND THE WORLD

*"Edward Panosian . . . was masterful, regal, wicked and wretched,
and he commanded the stage as much as his kingdom of Thebes."*

—Lucille B. Green[155]

Ed Panosian is an exceptional performer. That's not to say that there is anything artificial about the man. He is without guile. But every classroom lecture and every private conversation is engaged with passion and delivered with flair. Panosian doesn't tell stories—he *becomes* them, and he takes his hearers with him.

For that reason, you might assume that his acting career was inevitable—that a talent scout must have seen latent ability in young Ed. You would be wrong. Panosian got his first acting gig because "the shoe fit," so to speak.

Ed Panosian managed to complete his undergraduate education at Bob Jones University without performing in a single dramatic production. But when he was a graduate assistant, someone else's misstep became Ed's opportunity. A young man who had a significant role in the Classic Players' Shakespeare play managed to get himself expelled—"shipped" in BJU parlance. It happens. Panosian picks up the story:

---

[155] Lucille B. Green, "'Antigone' Skillfully Performed at BJU," *Greenville News* (Greenville, SC), 1965.

Eva Carrier was directing the play—*Henry IV.* I was a graduate assistant. The play had been cast, and costumes had been made. And one player—a student—was shipped in the midst of rehearsals. The director had to have somebody who would fit the costume! That was the only criterion! I fit the costume, so I got the part. And that was my theatrical debut! Not for talent or ability, but for girth!

Almost crying with laughter, I told him, "That is a *great* story." He laughed even more loudly and bellowed, "It's *true!*" In God's humorous providence, a graduate assistant named Ed was introduced to the stage because another lanky student was sent packing. In time, the stage would captivate Panosian, and he in turn would captivate audiences.

While he may have been out of his depth for a time, Panosian learned to act from masters of the craft. BJU film producer Katherine Stenholm was a rare talent, so much so that she broke through the glass ceiling that limited women in the mid-twentieth century and was put in charge of Unusual Films, the university's cinema production division. Ed, like all students at BJU, had been required to take at least six hours of speech. He had benefited from basic speech and interpretation classes. But he learned to act on the job, both on the stage and the screen, under the direction of geniuses like Stenholm and Carrier.

Perhaps more importantly, Panosian learned to act under the watchful (and often critical) eye of Bob Jones Jr., the president of BJU from 1947 to 1971 and its chancellor until his death in 1997. Dr. Jones was a man of culture and an accomplished actor in his own right. As a young man, he studied with the Shakespeare Company in Stratford-upon-Avon, England, a respected institution and a highly sought-after opportunity. He gained acclaim in the United States for his "Curtain Calls," a solo Shakespeare program, and he was lauded by the International Lyceum Association as "the best young actor of Shakespeare in America."[156] Nevertheless, he eschewed opportunities for stardom, even declining the offer of a screen test and contract from Warner

---

[156] Turner, *Standing Without Apology,* 130. Lyceum clubs exist to promote culture and the arts.

Brothers Studios in Hollywood in 1937.[157] He opted instead for the calling to ministry, and he infused his zeal for drama and the arts into Bob Jones University. It was principally Bob Jones Jr. who shaped BJU into an elite academic and cultural institution. He refused to tolerate anything but the exceptional at the university that bore his family name, and that pursuit of excellence continues to be a hallmark of the school to this day.

In 1929, Bob Jones Jr. was instrumental in founding the university's Classic Players, a Shakespearean acting company which he led for many years and which continues annual performances almost ninety years later.[158] Even when he wasn't starring in or directing a play, he would often sit in the back of the massive Rodeheaver Auditorium and goad the actors during rehearsals. The Panosians fondly recall hearing his loud complaints: "I can't hear you. You might as well sit down if I can't hear you! Speak up!" There was no amplification system during performances, so the actors had to fill the theater with nothing but their own voices. Jones' "faithful wounds"[159] were motivating, inside the theater and out. Under Jones' benevolent despotism, Panosian—and everyone else—learned to enunciate and project. But they learned much more. Panosian and many of his contemporaries at BJU who became pillars of the institution rose to unimagined heights at Bob Jones Jr.'s insistence. His influence on Ed Panosian, first as a student, then as a faculty member and actor, was immense. Panosian's fondness for the man can hardly be exaggerated.

Ed Panosian would play lead roles in several Shakespearean plays. He played Caliban and Prospero in *The Tempest*. He was Duncan in *Macbeth*. He was Antonio in *The Merchant of Venice*. He was *Othello*. And, as earlier noted, Dr. and Mrs. Panosian enjoyed multiple opportunities to play the lead roles of rivals and eventual romantics Petruchio and Kate in *The Taming of the Shrew*, performing the roles in 1961,

---

[157] Turner, *Standing Without Apology*, 128.
[158] Turner, *Standing Without Apology*, 128.
[159] Proverbs 27:6.

1971, and 1981. Dr. Panosian deadpans, "I tell people that the taming of the shrew only lasts ten years; you have to redo it after ten years!" Once again, our laughter fills their small home.

The Panosians have a scrapbook which chronicles many of their most cherished memories. Family appears often, of course. But so does Shakespeare!

Ed as Hotspur in *Henry IV*, 1956; photo courtesy of Bob Jones University

Ed as Duncan in *Macbeth*, 2003; photo courtesy of Bob Jones University

Theater faculty member Lonnie Polson, who directed Dr. Panosian in the 1996 production of *The Tempest*, sent him the following
handwritten note, typical of many others in the scrapbook:

Dr. Panosian,

It has been an honor to work with you on *The Tempest*. Your performance is outstanding, and I have learned so much from watching
you act. Thanks also for your influence on the cast and for the dignity
and professionalism you brought to the production.

Sincerely,

Lonnie Polson

Dr. Bob Jones III, who shared the stage with Dr. Panosian on
multiple occasions, treasured the experience:

He was a Shakespeare interpreter par excellence. My wife and I had
the privilege of acting in several Shakespearean productions with
him. He was deeply submersed in his characters. When he was on
stage, something was "happening" between him and the other actors.

Dr. Darren Lawson, the current Dean of the School of Fine Arts
at BJU, was one of those "other actors." He learned much from Dr.
Panosian, the skilled, yet selfless actor:

Although I had Dr. Panosian for History of Civilization like thousands of others before and after me, I learned even more life lessons
from acting on stage alongside him in Rodeheaver Auditorium. He
was a commanding presence on the theatrical stage, but when it was
your turn to speak, he would position himself in such a way to "give"
you the stage in the most gracious manner. It taught me the importance of positioning myself in a way to feature others. I also greatly
appreciated his interest and support of the arts at BJU. He knew the
role it played in shaping our students to become better servants for
the glory of Christ.

Praise for Panosian's on-stage presence came not only from actors
and directors, but from critics. Reviews of his performances regularly
extolled his efforts:

A fine performance was turned in . . . by Edward Panosian as
Macduff, particularly in the final scene in Act IV when he learns of
the death of his wife and babes. In the forepart of the scene as he
talked with Malcolm, his voice rang out in patriotic fervor.[160]

---

[160] Lucille B. Green, "Actors Make 'Macbeth' Alive Again at BJU," *Greenville News* (Greenville, SC), May 27, 1967.

With impressive voice and diction, Edward Panosian was outstanding in the huge cast. He played the part of a Czech noble and served as narrator.[161]

It was Edward Panosian as Creon who dominated much of the 90-minute production, which ran without intermission. He was masterful, regal, wicked and wretched, and he commanded the stage as much as his kingdom of Thebes.[162]

In a typical display of self-deprecation, Dr. Panosian downplays his acting abilities. I told him that he performs so *naturally*, and he immediately shot back, with a laugh, "That's because I never learned to act!" He insists that acting was only a hobby for him, but one that he came to enjoy very much. In his mind, he succeeded as an actor for one reason: "God gave me a loud voice, and I can't take any credit for it, but I used it."

Ah, that "loud voice." Seeing Ed Panosian act was a privilege. He moved with dramatically long strides, always entering and exiting the stage with unmistakable purpose. But it was *hearing* him that called forth goosebumps. The late New York Yankees' public address announcer Bob Sheppard was said to have "the voice of God." With respect to Sheppard, no one speaks on behalf of deity more convincingly than Ed Panosian. He recorded voiceovers and performed narrations for countless concerts and vespers performances at BJU, often speaking lines which God once said.[163] One riveting sample of his peerless voice can be heard at the opening of a Christmas album titled *Rejoice*, produced in 1994. Listen to it but once, and you will henceforth be unable to read Luke 2:10–11 without hearing the booming voice of "Ed the Archangel" in your head: "Fear not, for, behold, I

---

[161] Gil Rowland, "What's Doing: BJU Drama Has Audience Breathless; May Provoke Argument," *Greenville Piedmont* (Greenville, SC), November 29, 1968.

[162] Lucille B. Green, "'Antigone' Skillfully Performed at BJU." *Greenville News* (Greenville, SC), 1965.

[163] Dr. Panosian's narrations appear on multiple products from BJU Press, including *Animals in the Bible* (DVD). He was also part of a radio cast which performed "The Battle of Bull Run" on WMUU and other stations in 1961. "'Battle of Bull Run' Aired," *Voice of the Alumni* 35, no. 2 (Sept. 1961): 2.

bring you good tidings of great joy, which shall be to all people. For unto you is born this day in the city of David a Saviour, which is Christ the Lord."[164]

Unusual Films, the movie-making branch of Bob Jones University, was in full swing during Panosian's tenure. His dramatic gifts translated with apparent ease onto the big screen. He appeared in movies spanning no less than seven decades: *Wine of Morning* (1955), *Flame in the Wind* (1971), *Beyond the Night* (1983), *The Printing* (1990), *The Treasure Map* (1999), and *Milltown Pride* (2011). The olive complexion he received from his Armenian forebears served him well as an actor, as he convincingly played a Spaniard, an African (with considerable makeup), a Russian, and a Native American.

Ed as Yakov in *The Printing*, 1990; photo courtesy of Bob Jones University

---

[164] *Rejoice: A Christmas Celebration for Choirs & Orchestration,* Sacred Music Services, compact disc.

Again, in God's sovereignty, just as Panosian's physique led to his career as an actor, Panosian's acting led to his far-reaching ministry of presenting first-person historical narratives. In 1983, Dr. Alan Cairns, a good friend of the Panosians and then the senior minister of Faith Free Presbyterian Church in Greenville, South Carolina, approached Panosian with a genius idea. He related how the famed preacher-politician of Northern Ireland, Ian Paisley, had attempted to do a presentation of the life of Martin Luther in first person. He stood in the pulpit, inhaled a massive breath, then boomed out in his thick Irish brogue: "I am Martin Luther!" It did not go over well.

There was too much Paisley in Ian for any other character to show through! But it sparked an idea for Dr. Cairns. Knowing that Panosian was an accomplished actor, and that his "day job" was teaching church history, Cairns suggested that he take up the challenge: why not try presenting the life of Reformer Martin Luther in character—*as Martin Luther?* This Panosian did, debuting the role in a service for Cairns' congregation. The positive response of the church exceeded both of their expectations.

Year by year, Luther was joined by others in the Panosian collection of biographical sketches: John Knox, the Scottish Reformer; John Calvin, the Reformer, author, and firebrand; William Tyndale, the Bible translator; John Wesley and George Whitefield, revivalist preachers; John Bunyan, the English tinker, preacher, and writer; Hugh Latimer, the English martyr; John Hus, the Bohemian martyr and pre-Reformer; and Charles Spurgeon, the Baptist preacher, educator, author, and all-around champion of Bible preaching.[165]

Ed Panosian knows he wasn't called to preach. But these first-person historical roles have allowed him to proclaim biblical truth and to effectively extend his ministry far beyond his retirement from BJU in 2004. He has taken his ten friends all over the United States, and he has exported them to almost every peopled continent in the world,

---

[165] Abridged versions of five of the biographical sketches—Luther, Tyndale, Knox, Bunyan, and Spurgeon—were released on DVD in 2003 by BJU Press.

including a trip to India in 2015 at the age of eighty-five. God has used them! And yet, even in his travels to teach, Dr. Panosian's humility was on display:

> I taught Russian pastors one summer, which was a humiliating experience. Some of them had been in concentration camps for the gospel, and I was teaching *them* church history. They had lived it! [His voice trailed off, strained with emotion.]

God stuffed an astounding amount of ability and energy into the man Ed Panosian. Fortunately, his body is tall and long enough to contain it—and still to fit into the costume that started it all.

CHAPTER TWENTY–THREE

THE BELOVED FATHER

1959–PRESENT — GREENVILLE, SOUTH CAROLINA

"Dr. Panosian challenged seminary students: 'Your home
ought to be a seminary. You're training an army for the Lord.
Change not the tone of your voice when the telephone rings!
Your marriage relationship must be nourished, not assumed!'"

—Joe Tyrpak[166]

The year 1959 was a banner year for Ed and Betty Panosian. In May, Ed completed his doctorate in Church History from BJU, including credits taken at other institutions. On November 15, 1959, they welcomed their first son to the world. It was one of the happiest times in their lives—and one of the most frightening.

Mark Edward Panosian was born ten weeks premature, weighing only two pounds, eleven ounces. It wasn't at all clear that he would survive. Dr. Panosian shares, "The doctor came to me and said, 'Mr. Panosian, you have a son—but we don't know how long he will be with us.'" If the boy did survive, it wasn't at all clear that he would be free of ongoing complications. Dr. and Mrs. Panosian had already endured the sadness of several miscarriages. They braced themselves for another sorrow.

The Panosians prayed that Mark would live. By God's grace, he did. The Panosians prayed that he would be healthy. By God's grace, he was.

---

[166] Joe Tyrpak is the lead pastor of Tri-County Bible Church in Madison, Ohio. He authored the Christian history devotional and documentary *The Life of David Brainerd* and is a contributor to the *Gospel Meditations* devotional series. He is also the artistic editor of this book.

God is the ultimate Multi-Tasker. He uses our trials to increase our faith and improve our character. But He also uses them to prepare us for future ministry to others, allowing us to pass on the comfort we ourselves have received.[167] The Panosians were able to utilize their own experience with baby Mark in ministry to others, as Dr. Michael Barrett[168] shares:

> I did not have Dr. Panosian much as a teacher, but one thing he did will never be forgotten. Our son Charlie was born several weeks early and had several close calls in which we thought we would lose him. This would have been my first year as full-time faculty. I remember one day, when we were particularly concerned over a new crisis, that Dr. Panosian came to me offering whatever help he could give, including covering some of the hospital expenses. He shared with us that they had a similar situation with their son Mark and knew what we were going through. I have forgotten most of what he taught in that one semester of church history, but I have never forgotten his genuine kindness and concern.
>
> By God's grace, Charlie did survive—like Mark had before him. Ironically, he grew to love church history because of Panosian. Charlie would have licked the dirt off the man's shoes.[169]

The Panosians had been entrusted with a young life, and they were both relieved and thrilled to be parents. Their lives were incredibly busy, but very fulfilling. Ed continued his normal teaching regimen. Betty balanced being a young mother with part-time teaching in the speech department, relying on daycare from the university when she was in class. As if life for the young family weren't busy enough, 1961 was the year when the couple debuted as Petruchio and Kate in *The Taming of the Shrew.*

They were expecting again a short time later, in 1963. Because of the early arrival of Mark, Mrs. Panosian's doctor wanted to protect against another premature birth. He prescribed a common drug

---

[167] 2 Corinthians 1:3–4.

[168] Dr. Michael P. V. Barrett was a long-time Old Testament professor at BJU. He has also served as the president of Geneva Reformed Seminary in Greenville, SC, and is now Vice President for Academic Affairs and an Old Testament professor at Puritan Reformed Theological Seminary in Grand Rapids, MI.

[169] Dr. Charles Barrett's appreciation for Dr. Panosian is shared on page 145.

believed to promote a longer pregnancy: diethylstilbestrol. Grateful for anything that would promote the baby's health, Betty began taking the medication. However, the drug nauseated her so much that she was unable to continue taking it. She opted instead for bed rest. Betty spent a good part of the summer of 1963 in the old BJU hospital—what is now one side of the quadrangle of Bob Jones Academy. "She lived on her back for most of three months," Panosian recalls. Despite their tight budget, Ed purchased a window unit air conditioner for his wife's hospital room, doing what little he could to make her more comfortable during the hot Carolina summer. The air conditioning unit would stay in the room long after Betty's departure, a contribution for which patients in subsequent summers would be grateful.

Lisa Noel Panosian arrived on September 23, 1963—four weeks early, but healthy. Her parents were thankful, but they didn't yet realize how blessed they had been. A few years later, in 1971, it was discovered that diethylstilbestrol was extremely dangerous. Dr. Panosian explains:

> Later, it was discovered that that medicine led to birth defects. And if she had continued to take it, the expectation was—medically—that it would have been a problem to the baby. And that baby was Lisa, who is a jewel. She is just a godly girl, and a blessing, and she has been to many people. But whatever she is, it was the providence of God that caused Betty to get ill taking the medicine, long before it was known that it was causing birth defects. That is a beautiful history to remember. The Lord is good.

Once again, God's providence had been uniquely displayed in the Panosians' lives, this time using nausea—a seeming burden rather than a blessing—to prevent what might have been immeasurably worse.

Six years later, the final of the Panosians' three children arrived. Matthew Ian Panosian was born on December 31, 1969, four weeks early, and just in time to give his parents a tax deduction. Once again, the Panosians rejoiced at the birth of a healthy child. BJU alumnus and faculty member Connie Collins recalls the beginning of the spring semester in January of 1970. Dr. Panosian was still exultant over Matthew's arrival: "He came into class so excited, handing out Tootsie Rolls to everyone. There was applause!" Reminded of this event, Dr. Panosian deadpans, "Well, there were no cigars in the campus store."

The Ed Panosian family, 1974; left to right: Mark, Matthew, Ed, Betty, and Lisa

As was the policy at BJU at the time, Betty continued working part-time despite having young children. The university had been able to keep prices low for students in part due to a voluntary "communal living arrangement" with its faculty and staff, not unlike the "kibbutz" model in Israel. Housing was provided. Meals were provided. Healthcare was provided. Modest salaries were provided. And future retirement was promised. As a result, couples would agree to join the staff as a "team." Mothers worked less than they had before having young children, but they did work on campus.

During one of our interviews together, I asked Mrs. Panosian if it was difficult to continue a fairly full teaching load despite being a

mother: "Did you want to be home with the children?" She replied
with an honest, but discreet answer: "Some days." At that point, her
husband interjected: "Other days you were glad to be rid of them!" As
often happened during our talks, that sentence was punctuated by a
great laugh that filled the room. Her response was more subdued, but
still comical in her understated fashion: "Well, I had two boys. Lisa
was a princess, but the boys were *not!*" Once again, laughter ensued.

Mrs. Panosian had two boys. On occasion, it may have seemed like
she had three. BJU alumna Nancy Lohr tells what a whimsical father
Dr. Panosian could be, relying on the testimony of an eyewitness:

> I took Storytelling with Mrs. Panosian, and she shared that when
> Dr. Panosian told *Little Red Riding Hood* to their youngest son,
> he wore a red kitchen towel as his hood. The image has remained
> endearing over the years.

Those who have seen Dr. Panosian narrate *Peter and the Wolf* can
imagine what a dramatic performance Dr. Panosian must have given
as a girl, her grandmother, a wolf, and its hunter!

———

Betty Panosian's life with Ed has been a grand adventure. Their
ministry has taken them all over the world, and they have had wonderful experiences. When she has felt a twinge of timidity, his bravado has
been enough for them both. One example, shared by Betty, will suffice:

> I can remember we went to the World Fair when it was in New York
> City. And they had the *Pietà* there.[170] They had a lovely royal blue
> velvet behind it. Most people had to go by it on escalators—slow-
> moving sidewalks. But there was one level with a great view, right
> near it. But a sign was posted: "Only Nuns and Priests" were allowed
> to stand down there. And my husband tells me, "We're going down
> there." I said, "Honey, the sign says it's just for nuns and priests."
> And he said, "I am a saint!" [The proclamation is accentuated by her
> laughter.] And so there we were, looking at the *Pietà*. And here I
> am—I'm always the rules person—and I was ready to leave, waiting

---

[170] The *Pietà* is a fifteenth century marble sculpture by Michelangelo.

for them to throw us out! But no one did. And he got to drink his fill of the *Pietà*. [More nostalgic laughter.]

Life for the Panosians, however, was not always comical. Betty Panosian has struggled throughout her life with Crohn's disease, at one point necessitating a surgery to remove a portion of her intestines. She has had other health troubles as well, and she has handled them with grace.

In 1992, her husband faced his own health crisis. I recall campus prayer requests being made for Dr. Panosian, who was sixty-two years old at the time. After a normal breakfast, Panosian felt unwell. He had a strange sensation in his arms and chest; he was having a heart attack. He went first to Barge, the on-campus hospital that was intended to handle minor health needs. From there he was sent downtown to St. Francis Hospital. He had open heart surgery—a double bypass. The campus of faculty, staff, and students prayed for his safety and recovery. By God's grace, the surgery was successful.

However, it was not final. In 2005, at the age of seventy-four, Dr. Panosian had a second heart attack. He was awakened in the middle of the night with severe chest pains. This time, an ambulance rushed to his back-campus home and took him again to St. Francis Hospital. For a second time, Dr. Panosian had open heart surgery—this one a triple bypass. Also for a second time, the surgery was successful. Dr. Panosian now wears a pacemaker for added assistance.

Dr. Panosian has fully recovered and has no limitations related to his heart. Alumnus Mark Ward describes Dr. Panosian's age-defying fitness: "I remember watching Dr. Panosian at some unspecified age over seventy going up the stairs in the Alumni Building two at a time while wearing classy plaid pants."

Now eighty-eight, Dr. Panosian limits himself to but one stair at a time. But he continues to walk regularly for his enjoyment, for his health, and as a service to his less mobile wife. Sara Eilert, a student who quietly observed his comings and goings at the Dining Common during her time at BJU in recent years, shares the impression his patient walks from back campus made on her:

> Multiple times a week, I would pass Dr. Panosian on the sidewalk by the girls' dormitories or see him in the Dining Common carrying meals in disposable dishes. His pace was slower than the college students rushing to eat and get to class, but he was so consistent in his routine that I noticed. Often in the middle of the Dining Common, BJU retirees would meet for meals and fellowship, but I never saw Dr. Panosian join them. Instead, he took food home to Mrs. Panosian. The majority of more recent BJU students and graduates did not have Dr. Panosian as a teacher; however, we did see a faithful and caring husband serving his wife on a daily basis.

Ed Panosian's love for his wife has been evident to all who have seen them together. Many have commented to me how much they enjoyed watching him open the door for her, or seeing them holding hands as they walked around campus. There's a story behind that, from the camp where young Ed Panosian became a Christian. He shares:

> During the same week of camp when I trusted Christ, I was observing a fifty-year-old couple from my church during an evening session. It was an evening preaching service and I, as a fifteen-year-old boy, saw these two ancient adults sitting there listening to the message, holding hands. I liked that. I thought that was beautiful. Here are these old people who have been married all these years, and they still are in love. In my youthful idealism, I said, "I want to be like that." It left an impression. They never knew it, but it left an impression.

Many years later, the "ancient" Panosians have left a similar impression on countless others. Dr. Bob Jones III, who worked with them for many years on stage as well as on campus, expresses the influence Dr. Panosian has had on those who would graduate and begin their own families:

> He was never in a hurry, but deliberate and measured when speaking, walking, or bicycling across the campus. Dignity and decorum in all things were his trademark. He and his wife, Betty, revealed their love and care for each other when in public, as marital love should. They were teaching students yet to be married about what Christian love and respect in marriage should look like.

The Panosians have special relationships with each of their children in their adulthood. All three of them now live in the Greenville, South Carolina, community. Mark, who shows no evidence of his uncertain beginning, works as a credit manager for Synnex Corporation, an international computer supplier. Lisa, who studied German at BJU, works as a systems support specialist for a German company, Draexlmaier Automotive. Matthew is the Chief Credit Officer for Accord Financial, a company which serves as a factor, funding accounts receivables for companies to assist cash-flow.

All three of the Panosian children know the Lord as their Savior, for which their parents are unspeakably grateful. Matthew's salvation came by a special work of God, following several years as a prodigal. He freely shared with me that he was rebellious during his teen years, and that his resistance to authority eventually got him expelled from Bob Jones Academy. (As far as I know, he didn't leave behind a role or costume for a budding thespian.) It was a painful experience for him and for his parents, but God used it for good. Matthew returned to BJU for his college years, but it was *after* his graduation from BJU that he was born again by faith in Christ. He is grateful for God's patience and persistence, and he prays that his experience will be an encouragement to others. Dr. Panosian speaks of him with deep emotion and gratitude: "He is a godly young man, and he is rearing his three sons to be godly young men. He is a miracle of grace!"

Dr. and Mrs. Panosian have been blessed with five grandchildren and two godly daughters-in-law. Mark's wife is Oonagh (Shultz) Panosian; their children are Nazar (named after his great-grandfather) and Ghevont, the Panosians' only granddaughter (another Armenian name, acknowledging their heritage). Oonagh is a reading specialist, and she taught special education in public schools for several years. She now tutors schoolchildren in her home. Matthew's wife is Amy (Price) Panosian, a visual artist and art teacher and the mother of three more boys: Ethan, Ben, and Micah. Dr. and Mrs. Panosian are justly proud of and grateful for their quiver of grandkids. The entire family—children and grandchildren, like their parents and grandparents—are trophies of God's grace. As Dr. Panosian is fond of saying, "The lines have fallen unto me in pleasant places" (Psalm 16:6).

Dr. Panosian is a celebrity in his relatively small circles. Thousands of former students, most unknown by him, feel a special kinship to him. But he is more than a public figure.

He is a loving and attentive husband to his wife. He joyfully cares for Betty and eagerly praises her.

The Ed Panosian family, 2015; back row, left to right: Matthew, Amy, Ethan, Ghevont, Nazar, Lisa, Oonagh, and Mark; front row, left to right: Micah, Ed, Betty, and Ben

He is a proud and devoted father to his children. He is justifiably gratified by his children's accomplishments. He is profoundly grateful for their faith in Christ.

He is an adoring and doting grandfather to his grandchildren. To them, he isn't a larger-than-life professor or an actor with a dramatic and resounding voice. He's just "Grandfather." As he should be.

CHAPTER TWENTY–FOUR

"I SPEAK AS A FOOL"

ALMOST ALWAYS —
GREENVILLE, SOUTH CAROLINA

"A merry heart doeth good like a medicine."

—Proverbs 17:22

Ed Panosian is in blood earnest when he stands behind a lectern or pulpit. He treats teaching opportunities as a sacred trust, and he stewards them well. But he also has a savory wit, and he liberally dishes it into his lectures to make potentially bland history lessons a bit more palatable. For those who pay attention, his lectures are filled with subtle, but often hysterical ironies. His humor isn't slapstick. It's smart. It's sophisticated, like him. Pay attention or you'll miss the joke!

He would often open a semester's class with his classic introduction: "Hello. I am Doctor Pa-*NOS*-ian. The emphasis goes on my dominant feature." At this point, he'd turn his head sideways to show his profile, then face forward again and deadpan, "But only I can say that." Such self-deprecating humor is still common from him, and it is winsome. In his classes, it served a purpose. The intimidating professor teased himself; the ice was broken; the students were his. "And," he adds, "they knew how to pronounce my name!"

At times, his disarming self-deprecation took place on the fly. Jennifer Hayes, a former student, relates a time when Dr. Panosian tripped and fell flat, in front of hundreds of horrified freshmen:

> While pacing back and forth across the stage in my History of Civ class, Dr. Panosian misstepped and fell rather spectacularly. Apparently unhurt, and sensing the concern in the deathly silent class, he bounced back up and gave a list of dates: "The fall of Rome: 476 AD!

The fall of Constantinople: 1453 AD! The fall of Panosian: 1990 AD!"

Another former student, Jim Davis, shares a memorable one-liner that served as an ice breaker on the first day of his class in 1997: "I am Dr. Panosian. I taught your parents History of Civ—[million dollar pause]—I will not teach your children History of Civ."

One of his favorite teaching tactics, even now, is to play the devil's advocate, arguing vehemently for a nonsensical position to demonstrate its utter folly. Those who know him will recognize that he's being facetious by his tone of voice, his raised eyebrows (either one or both), his quickened pace (as if urging the audience to hurry up and nod in agreement), and his exaggerated earnestness—all merging to show the position's supposed plausibility. If those unspoken cues don't suffice, you'll catch the irony from his final, frozen expression: his torso leaned forward, his head titled, his mouth slightly open, his jaw slightly crooked, and his tongue planted firmly—and quite literally—in his cheek. To remove all doubt that the position he has been representing is absolute rubbish, he invariably concludes his role-playing with a classic line he has borrowed from the apostle Paul: "I speak as a fool."[171]

Other times, he would deal with an error more dismissively by simply instructing his students to write "bologna" in the margin of their textbooks.

Quizzes and tests usually yield bad memories, but with Dr. Panosian, they became the stuff of legend. Frequently, he would wear an especially bold outfit on test days—often his famous plaid pants. Before the exam he would comfort the stressed students by assuring them, "This, too, shall pass." Occasionally he would add, "Whether or not *you* do remains to be seen!"

Upon completion of a quiz, he would bring some levity to the in-class grading regimen with his exaggerated answers to quiz questions. The correct answer, according to Dr. Panosian, wasn't "E." It was

---

[171] 2 Corinthians 11:23.

"EEEEEE," spoken apparently with great difficulty, as though the sound were being summoned from underground. The next correct answer wasn't "B." It was "BEE," spoken as a robust interjection—as abrupt as the "EEEEEE" was elongated. The sound absolutely erupted from his mouth, but only after his cheeks and lips bulged and burst like a bubble: "BEE!" Were the answers spoken in this way to remove the possibility of misunderstanding him or merely to amuse the students, who always responded with a hushed giggle? He never let on—which would have ruined the joke—but I always suspected it was a little of each. The more I've come to know him, the more certain I am that he was clowning around a bit, though I've still not collected enough courage to ask him directly. Panosian coyly adds this observation: "No one was ever unsure which letter I had pronounced."

He has a masterful ability to invent the perfect one-liner off the cuff. BJU alumna Anita Wells shares the following gem:

> I remember one vespers rehearsal. I was in an instrumental group. He was reciting a line about "death calling" when the stage phone rang. He said, "I don't know about any of you, but I'm not answering that."

Colleague Dr. Linda Hayner, in a speech delivered at Dr. Panosian's retirement banquet on February 6, 2004, related a funny story which I enjoyed too much not to include:

> On the Saxon settlement in England he waxed eloquent in explaining the geographic position of the Saxon kingdoms: "In the east, was Essex or the kingdom of the East Saxons; in the west, Wessex of the West Saxons; in the south, Sussex of the South Saxons. However, in the north there was no sex. . . ." All students snapped to attention, the proctor ran for the nearest exit to explode in laughter, and Dr. Panosian spent valuable lecture time trying to explain what he'd really meant to say. . . .

Paul Isaacs was a student in the class, and he tells the same story, punctuating it with the students' reactions: "The place went up for grabs!"

Hayner also recalled Dr. Panosian's comical aversion to technology during his teaching career: "On seeing some of his close friends and colleagues succumb to the lure of PowerPoint, he walked away, shaking his head and muttering, 'A word is worth a thousand pictures.'" Indeed.

Humor—not PowerPoint—sneaks its way into Panosian's lectures even now. He often has a twinkle in his eye, a pun on his tongue, and an enormous laugh that sneaks out before the joke is quite finished. He'll open a lecture in a church by instructing his hearers to "take out a half sheet of paper, please," just like when they were students—sixty-plus years ago, for some! He has a knack for irony when he teaches. But outside of the classroom? Around campus, he could be an absolute court jester! He would speak and act "as a fool," to repurpose his famous phrase. The esteemed professor loves a good gag.

Dr. Panosian was often seen riding around campus on an old-fashioned bicycle, not unlike the one used by Miss Gulch in *The Wizard of Oz*. Invariably, he had on a full suit and tie. The image of him on that bike was iconic enough that BJU recently sent out a brilliant invitation to Homecoming 2017 with a 1981 picture of Dr. Panosian cycling around campus and a simple caption: "We just made you miss History of Civ, didn't we?" Every alumnus who opened his mailbox and was greeted by the image involuntarily answered, "Yes!"

A common sight around campus, 1981; photo courtesy of Bob Jones University

An even better bike gag happened during Gold Rush Daze in the early 1990s. Gold Rush Daze was a fun-filled event that took over the campus once every four years. Professors served dorm students breakfast in bed. The entire campus engaged in crazy competitions on the ballfields. The day ended with a fireworks display, which commenced after a comedy show featuring the administration, faculty, and staff. In the middle of that year's comedy show, Panosian surprised and thrilled the student body by riding his famous bike down the aisles of Founders Memorial Amphitorium, meandering through several sections of seats, and eventually riding across the massive platform. The visual alone was hilarious, but it was made even better by John Williams' theme from *E.T.* being played on sound system, all leading up to a video showing the shadow of Panosian and his bike flying across the moon like the original *Extra Terrestrial.*

Another time, Panosian was convinced to participate in Epsilon Zeta Chi's dating outing. The theme of the event was "That's Amore!" The society utilized everything Italian, from the music to the menu. But the highlight of the evening was an appearance by Dr. Panosian. Someone managed to get him to agree to play the role of an Italian mobster. As the students waited on a sidewalk near Alumni Stadium, Panosian's long black sedan pulled up. He stopped the car, lowered one of the windows, and shouted a threat in an Italian accent. He then proceeded to spray the entire group with a prop tommy gun, sound effects and all. Once "the hit" was finished, "The Panosian Godfather" sped away.

In November of 1992, Panosian agreed to entertain the crowd at the annual soccer championship—the Turkey Bowl—by taking a penalty kick against one of the school's best goalies during halftime. Matt Herbster stood in the goal, defending it against the kicks from notable faculty members and administrators, including Guenter Salter, Tony Miller, Bruce McAllister, Dwight Gustafson, Jim Berg, Bob Jones III, and Ed Panosian. Most struck the ball with what soccer players disparagingly call a "toe hack." Only one or two actually made a goal. (Tony Miller had spent the morning of the game practicing—a fact that made Dr. Panosian chuckle when I recounted the story.) Panosian, Salter, and Gustafson were the "elders" of the group. They all missed, but they did stay upright, despite their dress shoes—much to everyone's relief. It was a riot, and it wasn't out of character for any of them. Reminded of the occasion, Dr. Panosian summarized the event in his familiar self-mockery: "That was the *total* of my soccer experience!"

Faculty member Dr. Kerry McGonigal recalls an occasion when Dr. Panosian's role as teacher and actor collided:

> I had Dr. Panosian for Church History the semester he was filming Unusual Films' *The Treasure Map*. He was playing the part of an Indian, Henry Little Elk. One day he walked into Church History class after coming from a recording session for the movie. He evidently didn't have time to change out of his costume. So, there he was—standing before his seminary pupils, the august Dr. Panosian in his hat-rimmed hair, pony tail, and Western get-up, complete with blue jeans hiked up to his belly. The first thing he said to us in his inimitable voice was: "Go ahead, laugh. Just get it over with. Laugh now. . . ." He said it in the same eloquent manner in which he taught about Martin Luther and the Reformation!

Dr. Panosian has a wonderful talent for saying something exquisitely funny—and at the same time teaching a valuable lesson. Faculty member Mark Vowels recalls one such experience from his freshman year in 1979:

> In Freshman Orientation he taught us how vocal tones communicated meaning. He pronounced the word "oh" about ten different ways, and each carried a different meaning based on the inflection of his voice. It was both funny and (apparently) memorable. Lesson learned: Be careful not only what you say, but how you say it.

One more example of Dr. Panosian's wonderful wit and the lessons it can teach will suffice. Alumna Rena Stiekes shares an experience that took place in Rodeheaver Auditorium in the mid-nineties:

> Dr. Panosian was the lead in *The Tempest*. I was an undergrad and a walk-on, so I spent a lot of time waiting in the wings. I had no idea he was reviewing his lines in the darkness, sitting quietly near where I was goofing around with other girls. I belched out loud, and only then did I notice him chuckling at our silly group. He said, "Oh, no worries. I do that quite often. . . . However, *my wife* does not." Point taken.

Dr. Panosian is the picture of dignity and grace. He's refined. He's all class. But he's also humble enough that he doesn't take himself too seriously. He laughs, and he shares the "good medicine" of laughter with others. We love him for it.

PART FIVE

"IN THE HOUSE OF THE LORD"

CHAPTER TWENTY-FIVE

NAZAR AND SARA

1975 & 1987 — ELMIRA, NEW YORK

"I go the way of all the earth."

—King David[172]

Our attention was diverted from Nazar and Sara Panosian in order to follow their son Ed to Greenville, South Carolina. Their own story continued in his absence, in Elmira, New York, where they became prominent citizens in their small hometown.

Nazar and Sara enjoyed their children and grandchildren. At times, Sara's "old country" ways were a bit startling to her daughter-in-law Betty—"the American" who had married Sara's precious son "Edvert." Matthew Panosian tells how his grandmother would show up at his parents' home with pots and pans, ready to cook her son all the good Armenian food he was missing out on because he hadn't married an Armenian. "She wasn't an ideal mother-in-law," he laughs. Fortunately, Betty Panosian laughs about it as well: "The father ruled the house; but the mother ruled all of the wives of her sons. And that's just the way it was in the old country. I don't know if I could have managed if we had lived close by; but, as it was, we saw them once a year or so."

Asked to comment on her father-in-law, Betty gushes with admiration:

> Ed's father didn't have much education, but he was a brilliant man, just a brilliant man. He came to this country with nothing; and of sheer will power and know-how, he would glean things. People

---

[172] 1 Kings 2:2, which alludes to David's approaching death.

would come to him—Armenian friends who were educated—and he would ask them, "All right, what stock are you buying now?" He could run a business!

Sara and Nazar Panosian, circa 1945

The "brilliant man"—Nazar Panosian—was a wonderful example of the American dream. A young immigrant who had been thrust out of his violent homeland and had completed only the third grade, he had "made it." In 1969, the company he had founded celebrated fifty years in business. The Elmira *Star-Gazette* ran a story heralding the milestone, describing both the success of the business and the story of its founder. Here it is in its entirety:

Armenian Refugee Found Success in America

In 1913, a 20-year-old Armenian youth left his native country in fear of Turkish persecution against the Armenians.

Behind him as he sailed to the United Sates was his livelihood, a shoe shop he operated in partnership with a younger brother. In front of him was an uncertain future.

Almost penniless and with no friends, he set out by train to Detroit, Binghamton and finally Elmira where he settled.

———

Today, Nazar Panosian, the Armenian refugee who became patriarch and founder of the family enterprise that bears his name, is helping celebrate the business' 50th anniversary.

Now 75, Panosian was honored Sunday at a special banquet for family, employees, and guests in commemoration of the little shoe repair shop that grew up.

The business which started in 1919 as a shop on S. Main St., today includes a shoe department store and apparel shops in Elmira, Horseheads, Corning, Sayre and the Mall.

The original shop was devoted to shoe repair, but with the introduction of work shoes, new shoe sales gradually became more important. Today, when it comes to shoes, new shoes are the sole business.

One by one, as Panosian's five children grew up, they joined in to help Manuel Panosian, the oldest of the children, now president of the enterprises. The other children are stockholders.

———

Panosian himself, now inactive in the business, sees the 50th anniversary not so much as a landmark to personal dedication and hard work but as an example of what America offers to its people, especially [those] who know what life is like in other countries.

"If I hadn't left Armenia when I did, I would be dead a long time now," Panosian said. Within a year after his departure he learned that Turkish authorities who ruled Armenia had driven the Armenians out of their homes, killed many and confiscated their property.

He never heard from his younger brother and assumes he was killed.

Intensely patriotic and deeply religious, Panosian is grateful for the opportunities he has had in the United States.[173]

Dr. Panosian looks backward to that momentous event and forward to the next, which is fast approaching: "I remember the fiftieth anniversary. It's going to be the one hundredth anniversary now, in 2019, and they're still in business!" Panosian's Shoes is now run by the third generation of Panosians. "Dad would have been so proud, as he was at the fiftieth anniversary, I remember."

Just over two years after the company's anniversary, on May 23, 1971, Nazar and Sara achieved fifty years of marriage. To celebrate, they welcomed friends and family to an open house at the home of Manuel, their eldest son and the namesake of Nazar's little brother who perished in the genocide. An article in the *Star-Gazette*, alongside their picture, honors them and gives a synopsis of their story:

> Both Armenians who immigrated from Syria when they were teenagers, they met in Binghamton and were married there on May 23, 1921. Their attendants were the bride's sister, Mrs. Rose Tashjian of Fresno, Calif., and Avak Arikian of Elmira.[174]

Rose, who had shared Sara's saddest day when both saw their father murdered, had also shared her happiest.

God blessed Nazar and Sara Panosian, and their family, and their business. Dr. Panosian tells of the development of their small shoe empire:

> What began in 1919 as "South Main Street Shoe Repair" gradually grew into "Panosian's Shoes." Later, as it added apparel and eventually eliminated shoe repair, it became "Mr. Panosian's." For a time, it

---

[173] Tom Hartley, "Armenian Refugee Found Success in America," *Star-Gazette* (Elmira, NY), May 6, 1969.

[174] "Panosians to Celebrate 50th Wedding Anniversary," *Star-Gazette* (Elmira, NY), June 1971.

expanded to thirteen stores. Today it consists of the flagship store, operated by Manny's son David and his staff. In addition, for several years, "Panosian's Home World," featuring furniture and appliances, was operated by my brother Stanley, also in Elmira.

When asked about his parents' relationship with Christ, Dr. Panosian gave the following answer:

> I never heard a testimony from either my mother or my father about their conversion. But from my earliest memory, I've known that they have known the Lord from long before their coming to the United States. They were godly people. I'd overhear my mother praying for her children—on her knees, *in Armenian!* The only thing I could understand was the names of my siblings and me!
>
> The Christian Missionary Alliance Church in Elmira was built next to my father's shop, on land my father gave them. When the doors of the church were open, we were there, always attired in our best clothes. My parents were faithful in their church attendance, and they passed that on to their children.

On June 30, 1975, at the age of eighty-one, Nazar Panosian entered eternity. He died of heart trouble. Dr. Panosian compares his father's circumstance with his own two heart surgeries and realizes that his father's life might have been prolonged by modern medicine.

The Star-Gazette once again ran an article recounting the end of Nazar Panosian's odyssey alongside a picture of the aged man, distinguished in his suit and wire-rimmed glasses, with a noticeably kind look on his face:

> Nazar Panosian of 715 Larchmont Road, the founder of Mr. Panosian's, died Friday. He was 81.
>
> Mr. Panosian, a World War I veteran, arrived in the United States in 1913 from his native country, Armenia. He had left in fear of Turkish persecution against the Armenians.
>
> He left behind him his business, a shoe shop he operated in partnership with his brother.
>
> He settled in Elmira and became the patriarch and founder of the family business that bears his name. The business is over 50 years old....

Mr. Panosian was intensely patriotic and deeply religious, attending Hillcrest Baptist Church.[175]

On March 2, 1987, Sara Panosian joined her husband in glory. She died of cancer at the age of eighty-five.

Dr. Panosian reflects on their stories with humble wonder. Had either of them perished . . . had Sara's mother been cut open as one soldier had suggested . . . had Nazar not sailed to the United States when he did . . . had German missionaries not evacuated Sara and her siblings to Beirut . . . had Emma not sent her Uncle Dick to search for them . . . In short, had thousands of seemingly minor details not aligned just so, "there would have been no Panosian story," as Dr. Panosian puts it. "God is good. Again, providence."

Nazar and his bride Sara survived the very worst of which humanity is capable. They built a life together. They built a business together. They built a family together, raising five children and enjoying twelve grandchildren. And they did it as deeply grateful Americans.

Nazar—the boy with the egg, who had lost his mother and his younger brother. Sara—the girl with the pin cushion, who had lost her father and her older brother. They were overcomers. Survivors. Trophies of God's providence and grace.

Both enjoyed long, full lives, dying over sixty years later than their Turkish oppressors intended. Their vengeance for the unspeakable atrocities of the Armenian Genocide was *to live.* And having done so—successfully by every conceivable measure—they greeted death as a friend, not a foe. Because of their faith in Jesus Christ, both live on.

Their triumph is complete.

---

[175] "Nazar Panosian Dies," *Star-Gazette* (Elmira, NY), n.d.

CHAPTER TWENTY-SIX

THE PANOSIAN LEGACY

2004–PRESENT — GREENVILLE, SOUTH CAROLINA

"Ye are our epistle written in our hearts,
known and read of all men."

—2 Corinthians 3:2

"For what is our hope, or joy, or crown of
rejoicing? Are not even ye in the presence of
our Lord Jesus Christ at his coming?"

—1 Thessalonians 2:19

One volume is insufficient to summarize such a full life. It gives glimpses and snapshots, but it cannot possibly do justice to a life like Edward M. Panosian's. A biography is merely a scrapbook which holds a few treasured memories.

This book is a scrapbook turned to prose—quite literally. During my interviews with Dr. Panosian, I asked if he had any files or newspaper clippings that would help me go back in time a bit regarding some of the significant times of his life. He told me he had a scrapbook he would be happy to share with me. I was honored that he trusted me with it, as it was clearly important to his family.

As I perused its contents, I realized why it was so precious. It reminded me of his mother's pin cushion in that it contained priceless mementos from a storied past. In the scrapbook I found newspaper articles announcing the conferring of his doctorate, reviewing his Shakespeare performances, and celebrating the fiftieth anniversary of his father Nazar Panosian's shoe business. I found his father's obituary.

There are birth announcements of his children. It contains notes of gratitude from various Classic Players directors, from Mrs. Bob Jones Sr., from Bob Jones Jr., from Bob Jones III, and from BJU vice president Bob Wood. I even found a bookmark which had been given to "Eddie" Panosian in 1937 by his Sunday School teacher when he was only seven years old. I was walking through the best moments of his life, and I was overwhelmed by the kindness of God in giving us a man like Ed Panosian.

Ever since Panosian's graduation from high school in 1948, his story has been inseparable from the story of BJU. His legacy is tied to the school's. This is clear not only from numerous anecdotes shared by former students, but from the role he has played during some of the university's most significant times. Specifically, Dr. Panosian was trusted to be the voice of the university during the funeral services for Dr. Bob Jones Sr. and for Dr. Bob Jones Jr.

Bob Jones Sr., the founder of Bob Jones University, entered eternity on January 16, 1968, at the age of eighty-four. His memorial service was a solemn spectacle, attended not only by grateful alumni, but by civic and religious leaders from around the United States. His son, Bob Jones Jr., wrote a beautiful tribute to his father. However, he did not trust himself to read the statement in public on a day of such deep emotion. Instead, Bob Jones Jr.—one of the great orators of his generation—tapped Ed Panosian to speak on his behalf. The honor was not lost on the young faculty member, who was then only thirty-seven years old. It was a powerful combination—the words of a grateful and eloquent son, read by a man with an incomparable voice and inimitable expressiveness. Dan Salter, the son of the late dean and faculty member Dr. Guenter Salter, describes the moment in vivid detail as he learned it from his parents: "Dr. Panosian delivered as expected—with that perfectly relaxed cadence, carrying everyone listening in mesmerized measure through emotion, remembrance, and upward to glory."

In Dr. Panosian's treasured scrapbook is the program from the service, along with a published version of the speech, titled "A Tribute and a Pledge." Asked about the difficulty of reading such a moving

statement on such a timeless occasion, Dr. Panosian gave the following answer:

> Reading it in public was a spiritual experience for me. I remem-
> ber, while practicing reading it aloud the previous day, that I could
> not get through it without losing my composure. The Lord gave
> unusual strength during the funeral, as I got through it with His
> grace for the only time it mattered.

A generation later, when Bob Jones Jr. departed this life to be
with the Lord, it was once again Ed Panosian who served as one
of the spokesmen for a grateful people. The date was November 17,
1997. This time Dr. Panosian, representing the faculty and staff, spoke
words he had penned himself; they appear below in their totality
(emphases his):

> While all who hear these words must know the mortality of men,
> this "last of life for which the first was made" now permits us these
> moments to reflect on the life of Robert Reynolds Jones, the second
> of that name.

> At the time of the Founder's death, now thirty years ago, he whom
> we remember today said, "This should not be a day for weeping.
> This is a time for rejoicing. This should not be a moment for sorrow.
> This is an hour for gladness." Those were his words, and they are
> true now, as well. Yet now, as then, such is our human frailty that
> it is only with halting words that we speak the thoughts of these
> weeks and hours since first we considered the coming of this day.

> I represent this morning the faculty and the staff of this institution,
> which Dr. Bob Jones Jr. shepherded successively as acting Presi-
> dent, President, Chancellor, and Chairman of the Board. Each of
> us has known him in different generations and in different roles:
> some as an adopted grandfather, some as a second father, some in
> his office, some at table, some through notes and memos, some on
> Rodeheaver stage, some at the Art Gallery, some in films or radio,
> some as poet or architect, or author, or counselor, or teacher, some
> in other ways—Yet all of us have known him as preacher, exhorter,
> eloquent defender of truth, and friend.

> His fourscore and six years, his consistent ministry and exemplary
> godliness, his gentle firmness, and private tenderness have left
> indelible marks on the lives and labors of thousands. We shall not
> know the final harvest of his sowing "'til all the ransomed church of

God be saved to sin no more." We must not ascribe unto him praise he would not himself have accepted, for he knew that all praise belongeth to the God who enableth His servant to be His instrument; yet today he is due our gratitude for his dedicated use of his extraordinary gifts to the glory of God. It is not in man to measure the service of *God's* servant. His record is on high.

A man is known by his enemies as well as by his friends. Some feared Dr. Bob. Some hated him. Some are happy to see him out of the way. Yet we, with the thousands of others who loved him, know that he cared most that men should love his Savior and be obedient to the Sacred Book.

We pledge anew the continuation of his defense of "the faith once delivered to the saints," and both the maintenance and the extension of the testimony of this university which he so nobly personified for so many years. We call upon all who have stood with him to stand yet, and "having done all, to stand."

We thank God for him; we honor his Lord for having lent him to earth and now having received him into glory, the glory that awaits every blood-washed believer in Christ's finished work at Calvary. (What an abundant entrance must have been his that Wednesday morn!) *We* cannot really commend him to heaven; for the only commendation which holds in that place is his identification in Christ, and *His* righteousness.

Let me say to his dear wife, and sons, and daughter, and grandchildren, and great-grandchildren, and to all their families: We, the faculty and staff of Bob Jones University, commend to your souls the Balm of Gilead, with the psalmist's assurance that "weeping may endure for a night, but joy cometh in the morning."

And this final, personal word: Dr. Bob Jr. was eighteen years old when I was born. I was eighteen when I first met him. In that half-century since, he has been a faithful, true, and compassionate mentor and friend, who—as the apostle Paul exhorted Titus—has "adorn[ed] the doctrine of God our Savior."

We shall miss him.

And so, farewell, Dr. Bob. Today we bless God for you; and, one day, we shall bless God *with* you.

Ironically, Dr. Panosian concluded his moving tribute with the final lines from the movie *Sheffey*, one of only a few movies from Unusual Films in which he himself did not appear. The words for this august occasion were handwritten on 3x5 cards in all caps. The final words of some lines are bent ninety degrees to fit on the cards; the words of another line are added below and circled, with an arrow pointing to their intended location. I smiled as I read them and thought, "Abraham Lincoln would be proud." My smile turned to a chuckle when I looked on the back side of one of the index cards which held the speech and saw the writing of a former student:

Supportive Reading: Schaff, *History of the Christian Church,* 76 pages.
Text Reading: Yes, I read the assigned reading.
Time Spent: @ 6 hours.

Reading Dr. Panosian's eloquent tribute to Dr. Bob Jones Jr., one wishes he had had the liberty to write more. He wrote capably for publications from BJU, contributing articles to several editions of *Biblical Viewpoint*[176] and *The Voice of the Alumni.*[177] He wrote several chapters for books from BJU Press, such as *Faith of Our Fathers: Scenes from Church History* and *The Providence of God in History.* And he authored several scholarly booklets, including *The World Council of Churches* and *Islam and the Bible: Considering Islam Biblically.*

Dr. and Mrs. Panosian are part of the fabric of Bob Jones University. They love the school more deeply than people who came after them can understand. Ours is a generation devoid of brand loyalty. The Greatest Generation was different. "Griping will not be tolerated," was a mantra on the campus, affixed to the back of every dorm room door. There was a zero tolerance for disloyalty. Disagreement was fine—but not disloyalty. The Panosians were unflinchingly loyal to BJU. They still are.

Despite their considerable gifts, which surely would have led to monetary success in business or at public universities, the Panosians were content to live modestly in order to serve the Lord at BJU. It's not true that Dr. Panosian worked for free, or even for $1 a year.

[176] *Biblical Viewpoint* was a journal published biannually by the School of Religion faculty of Bob Jones University and Seminary from 1967 to 2005.
[177] *The Voice of the Alumni* is the periodical of the BJU Alumni Association. It was published from 1955 to 2010.

That's urban legend, as believable as it may seem to people. But like so many of their generation, they have been content to live in a modest back-campus home for over fifty years. Even now, they refuse to say a negative word about the university. Indeed, they are almost defensive of the wages they earned. Dr. Panosian, his voice rising with conviction, insists, "Our needs were always supplied. We were never in want. And the university has always given to its employees *more* than they promised—never less! And it was a *ministry!*"

Ed and Betty Panosian, 2013; photo by Derek Eckenroth, courtesy of Bob Jones University

Twenty-three years earlier, he expressed the same devotion to the school: "And this has been our home, and calling, and ministry, and joy, and privilege, and mission, and delight, and burden."[178]

Although Dr. Panosian is reticent to speak of money, his wife shares her deep admiration for her husband, his contentment, and his provision for their family:

---

[178] Turner, *Standing Without Apology,* 296.

If he had gone into business, as his brothers all did, I mean [she laughs], I'm sure he'd be in the Fortune 500. And maybe it would have been terrible. But he—he just was so smart; and living here on our salary, which was very little—I mean, for a time it was $150 a month for both of us, full-time—I marvel. . . .

But we never lacked. And he was always figuring out how [to make ends meet], because he would say, "I could go to my father, but I'm not going to." And we managed. I remember once something that pleased him so much, because all of his siblings lived in gorgeous homes, and have always had a lot of this world's goods—but his father said to him one day, "Edvert, you're the wealthiest of them all!" And I think that's true.

She gives one endearing example of how they survived—even thrived—on so little:

He has always had high tastes. He doesn't like things that are inexpensive. He likes a sale; but he goes immediately to the most expensive things. [She laughs.] We were in Spain, walking, and I saw his face light up. There was a Savonarola chair there. It had a leather seat and a leather back. And he said, "You know, let's go in and see how much that is!" So we went in, and we didn't see the comma [she laughs], and it was way beyond anything we could afford. But when we returned home, I went to [our friend and colleague] Earl Nutz and said, "Do you think you could make a chair?" And he went up to the art gallery and looked at the Savonarola chairs, and he made one. Earl just had an artist's hand with wood. And I gave it to Ed for Christmas. I have never seen him so happy!

The Panosians are models of simplicity and serenity. But it is not contentment with meager compensation that defines Dr. Panosian's legacy at BJU. Nor is it loyalty, as admirable as that quality is. It's not the fact that he was entrusted to give eulogies for the school's first two presidents. Dr. Panosian's legacy is his relationships with his students and with his Savior. His love for people and for Christ will linger long after he has gone to his reward.

Dr. Panosian has taught more students than anyone in BJU's history. With very few exceptions—including those who took History of Civ in summer school from local community colleges and thereby robbed themselves of a quintessential part of being a student at BJU—almost every student at the institution for a forty-year span sat under

Dr. Panosian's ministry. It left a mark on them. And it left a mark on *him*. Whether he was conscious of it or not, I noticed that whenever we discussed his former students he spoke not of "BJU graduates," but of "*our* graduates." In deep ways, even in his own mind, his life is inseparably intertwined with the ministry where he has served and lived for the last seventy years. His legacy is *people*.

Joe Henson III, the grandson of Dr. Panosian's colleague and dear friend Dr. Joe Henson Sr., shares his boyhood memories of Dr. Panosian:

> I was always impressed with his love of Scripture, his sense of humor, his concern for others, and his clarity of thought. As a teacher, he was evidently burdened to teach his students to think biblically and clearly.

Many former students who shared with me their memories of Dr. Panosian highlighted his humility. Carey Blough writes, "Although a larger-than-life character, Dr. Panosian was one of the most humble, down-to-earth servants of God I have ever known." Emmitt L. Wallace supports that commendation with a personal example:

> I had the privilege of being Dr. Panosian's chauffeur while he was in Maine conducting his *Church History in First Person* seminar. On one of our trips, he was helping my daughter with her times tables. I will never forget that: a great college professor who cared enough to relate well to an elementary student.

Judy Hoffman calls him "a gentleman's gentleman." Daniel Bannister concurs, recounting an incident that demonstrates Dr. Panosian's almost comical thoughtfulness:

> A couple of years after I graduated, I wrote a few of my favorite teachers thank you notes for their efforts at teaching and loving their students. A few weeks later, I received a thank you note from Dr. Panosian thanking me for my thank you note. You can never "out-polite" Dr. Panosian.

As important as the knowledge he imparted to his students were the lessons he himself embodied. Dr. Panosian is sophisticated without being pretentious. His friendly formality, his refined manners, and his precise way of speaking all served as an example to his students. Mark Ward expands on this idea:

Dr. Panosian came from an era in which verbal eloquence did not mark you off as elitist, but merely as respectful and educated. I always appreciated the self-conscious diction that accompanied his amazingly sonorous voice. I felt in his speech respect for the Lord, for me, and for the subject matter at hand. This, combined with his evident knowledge of his field, made him a larger-than-life figure.

Of course, we won't have Dr. Panosian forever. When I asked him about his closest friends, he replied, "Most of my friends and colleagues are in heaven." He said this with a chuckle, but it was unmistakably nostalgic and sad. The Panosians themselves will be in heaven in the relatively near future—a reality that has motivated me to finish this book now, while we can still express to them our appreciation. Greenville native and BJU alumnus Nathan Arnold expresses our eventual loss keenly:

Dr. Panosian is one of those ageless personalities that we know won't be with us forever, but who still seems to have almost paused in time. Even in his advanced years, he still carries himself with such dignity and grace. I appreciate him so much!

Paul Overly was a student of Panosian's, a colleague, and also a fellow worshipper at Faith Free Presbyterian Church. He writes:

Dr. and Mrs. Panosian have been part of our church fellowship for the last several years. Just his faithful presence has been a great blessing to me, but I have been especially blessed by the several times he has prayed aloud at our prayer meetings. He knows the Lord in a genuine, humble way.

The Panosians were part of BJU from its first year in Greenville. They watched the campus rise from the Carolina clay, one building at a time. And they were part of the building of the culture and values of the school itself—giving their entire lives to the cause of "the world's most unusual university."

But Dr. Panosian's legacy stretches beyond one institution. As deep as his ties are to BJU, Dr. Panosian has promoted something far greater. His is the legacy of a life lived *for Christ*. When Ed Panosian speaks of the Savior, he speaks of One he knows intimately. When he prays, he is speaking his native tongue. Dr. Panosian has shaped men and women because He himself has walked with God.

Dr. Panosian as Martin Luther in chapel at BJU in 2017, commemorating
the five hundredth anniversary of the Protestant Reformation; photo by
Derek Eckenroth, courtesy of Bob Jones University

Edward M. Panosian is a gentleman. An actor. A teacher. A husband. A father. An icon. But before all else, he is a *Christian*—and that has permeated everything he has done.

I can do no better than to allow Dr. Panosian to write his story's concluding lines himself:

> Throughout the narrative of this family's history, the principal theme has been the providence of our great God. Over and over He has shown Himself strong in our behalf, working providentially, powerfully, purposefully, and perfectly.

> And it is the continuing desire of the individual upon whom the book has focused, that the cry of the Psalmist be his: "Not unto us, O LORD, not unto us, but unto Thy name give glory" (Psalm 115:1).

> Ed Panosian rests, in time and in eternity, on Him Whom Charles Spurgeon called "the sovereign Arbiter of destiny, [Who] holds in His own power all the issues of our life."

> Spurgeon continued, "We are not waifs and strays upon the ocean of fate, but are steered by infinite wisdom towards our desired haven. Providence is a soft pillow for anxious heads, an anodyne for care, a grave for despair." And to this I say, "Amen."

TRIBUTES TO DR. PANOSIAN

"Render therefore to all their dues . . . honour to whom honour."

—Romans 13:7

A DAUGHTER'S TRIBUTE

by Lisa Panosian

If it is true that a child forms his first perception of the heavenly Father from his view of an earthly one, then my childhood perception of God—albeit imperfect, to be sure—was far more accurate than most. Being known as "Dr. Panosian's daughter" was never a burden to me; it was a delight, and it continues to be. Walking at my father's side across campus or into some assembly during those days gave me great pleasure. It still does. Solomon's declaration that "the glory of children is their fathers" is my own testimony.

Ed and Lisa Panosian at a baseball game during the 1996 Atlanta Olympics

I am overwhelmed at times by the realization that this gracious, godly gentleman—admired and treasured by thousands the world over—is, by God's good providence, my father. No one alive on earth today—except my dear mother, his beloved wife and closest companion of well over sixty years—knows him better or loves him more.

"We won't be perfect," my father wrote me in a letter some thirty years ago now, "but we can strive for perfect obedience to what we believe is right." This is how my father lives—and by both precept and example, he inspires me to endeavor to know and love the heavenly Father with an ever-increasing devotion.

STUDENTS' TRIBUTES
by Dr. David Fisher

Dr. Panosian taught history at Bob Jones University for more than fifty years. Through his godly testimony, keen mind, deep resonant voice, and passionate desire to convey God's truth and providential dealings, he has influenced the lives of thousands of students over the decades—including me. I had the privilege of sitting under his ministry both for my undergraduate and graduate degree programs.

Dr. Panosian epitomizes the "Renaissance" man whom he described so often when dealing with the Renaissance and Reformation periods—a man of many interests, many talents, and many accomplishments. He is well-known for his film, radio, and stage performances and is a sought-after speaker in churches and conferences. He is renowned for his masterful and inspiring first-person presentations of leading figures in church history.

A highlight of his teaching ministry was his ability to focus attention on God's providential dealings in the affairs of men and nations. "I have long believed," he used to say, "that if I can communicate to students the evidences of God's gracious oversight and His discernible interventions on men's behalf throughout history, they will be more confirmed in their confidence in His gracious care for them in every circumstance of life because of His providence."

He stressed the importance of a life grounded on the practical wisdom found in the Word of God and displayed on the pages of history. He admonished us to serve God in our calling, whatever it be; to live consistently, for few people do; to love people and use things—don't reverse it; to remember God is sovereign, we are His servants—don't reverse it; and to live for the right world, which is the eternal.

I am grateful to have sat under the "pulpit" of his classroom where he summarized what a man must know and thoroughly ponder: "God is great, and God is good; and thou, God, seest me." This gives both comfort and caution to a servant of God.

David Fisher has ministered at Bob Jones University for forty years, serving on the history faculty, as the Academy principal, as an author of history textbooks for BJUPress, and now as the vice provost for academic administration and the chief administrative officer. He holds a Ph.D. in church history, thanks in part to the influence of Ed Panosian. He speaks frequently at conferences promoting the cause of Christian education and God's providence in history.

---

by Dr. Tim Keesee

Many years ago, I was in Albania at a time when it was emerging from nearly fifty years under a brutal communist tyrant. When communism collapsed in 1990, there was no known church there—but that was about to change! During the early years of Gospel advance, a friend invited me to teach a series on church history to his little congregation of first-generation Christians. Night after night I shared the stories of faithful men and women—their brothers and sisters—who had followed Christ in their day, and it became clear to them that the Gospel they had heard and believed was the same one that Paul and Polycarp and Perpetua believed and died for. Their Bible was the same Scripture that Tyndale put into English and Carey translated into Bengali. They had been told by family and friends that they were deceived and were part of a cult, but now they saw the church was more than their little gathering—they were inseparably part of something worldwide and very wonderful.

I'll never forget the light in their eyes when all of this dawned on them. I recognized their joy because it was the same joy I first felt when I sat under Dr. Edward Panosian's church history lectures week after week. He was no partisan historian, no denominational cheerleader. Rather, he presented a Big Gospel view of the saving work that Jesus Himself started across the centuries and across the world as He gathered—and is gathering—His own from every nation and generation! I'll always be grateful for how Dr. Panosian pointed me to Christ, as my teacher, my colleague, and during some unforgettable days in Europe when we walked together in the footsteps of Luther, Zwingli, Calvin, and Wesley.

Tim Keesee is the Executive Director of Frontline Missions International and the author of Dispatches from the Front. *He was a student and later a colleague of Dr. Panosian.*

COLLEAGUES' TRIBUTES
by Dr. Ray St. John

"Commanding," "august," "masterly," "authoritative," "scholarly," "imposing," "dignified"—these and many more well-deserved adjectives tumble from the tongues of all who have known Dr. Ed Panosian. They give honor to a man we've admired from afar or from near at hand or perhaps from both. We've sat in Artist Series enthralled by his bringing to life a dashing figure like Petruchio, or in congregations challenged in spirit by his first-person accounts of a Martin Luther or a John Hus, or in classrooms almost overwhelmed by his command of and perspective on such broad subjects as the history of the world or the narrower historical epochs called the Renaissance and the Reformation.

Some of us have even had the pleasure of bantering with him in person as well as sitting in comfortable chairs conversing on topics that range from the state of the world to the state of the University. We've watched his tender, solicitous, patient attentiveness to his wife and family and felt humbled by his example. No matter the circumstance, we've been struck with his personal dignity and modesty, his delightful wit and wisdom, his spiritual depth and understanding.

For me personally, though, in none of these ways has he ever reached the stature he did one afternoon when in his office I fearfully confessed that, as a graduate student, frustrated with a low score on one of those ubiquitous "half sheets of paper," I had finessed an answer to gain a point I did not deserve. My conscience was stricken by my deceitful act, but on that day one of my heroes in the faith listened to my confession, then with gentleness and grace gave healing to my conscience. And for that, Dr. Ed Panosian—my teacher, my colleague, and my friend—I utter this tribute.

Ray St. John has been on the faculty of Bob Jones University for over fifty years. He is a respected author and editor, and he served as long-time chairman of the BJU English Department. He has pastored Trinity Baptist Church of Gaffney, South Carolina, since 1987.

by Dr. Ron Horton

I first encountered (a carefully chosen word) Edward Panosian as a freshman student at Bob Jones University when a group leader on the dormitory hall was collecting walk-ons for a Shakespeare performance in which he had a role. He thought my twin brother and I would benefit from the experience. The play was Shakespeare's *Henry IV*. The woman director was a stickler for detail. She must have thought hard about the casting, for she surely got it right. In all the nearly sixty years I've been on the teaching faculty, witnessing surely well more than a hundred performances of Shakespeare's plays, I've never seen one more astutely cast than this one. Prince Hal, later Henry V, was performed by Jack Buttram; King Henry IV by David Yearick; Owen Glendower by Grant Hendrickson; Falstaff by Dwight Gustafson; and memorably, Harry Hotspur, Earl of Northumberland, by Ed Panosian. It was Ed's first major role, but you'd never have known it. The fire, the swagger, the dash, the sheer delight with himself of this brash hero of the North in Ed's rendering galvanized the play. His dying words after defeat in personal combat with Prince Hal are unforgettable. "O Henry, thou hast robbed me of my youth."

Ed grasped the gist of every role I've seen him undertake and delivered it with dynamism, yet not without sensitivity to the needs of the play. As always, in everything he did on stage and off, he conducted himself with intelligence, style, and aplomb. I was in awe. I still am.

I was impressed with Ed's performance in History of Civilization, but captivated by his equally sculpted lectures in the two upper level courses I had from him. My interest in the European Renaissance and the Reformation was catalyzed then and would continue to grow throughout doctoral studies and subsequent teaching. They remain my primary academic area, and I relish opportunities, however rare, to return to it.

I was Ed's neighbor on the first-floor faculty office wing, along with Stewart Custer. We formed, I thought, a triad of scholarly interest in closely related fields. I remember joining him and Stu for an evening symposium in War Memorial Chapel on the topic of the Authorized (King James) Version of the Bible. Ed had the historical setting and process, Stu the scholarly achievement, and I, the rhetorical power. It was thought a memorable uniting of kindred minds. I, their junior, considered them my seniors in more ways than age.

I was impressed years later at a restaurant with Ed where he had invited me to lunch ostensibly to find out how I was handling the recent loss of my wife, Martha. I realized he was aiming even deeper, as a comforting friend, than just that.

"Manners maketh man" is a saying made proverbial by William of Wykeham, who adopted it as a motto for his coat of arms and for the two Oxford colleges, Westminster and New College, he founded in the late 1300s. Today, the saying is generally taken to refer to social polish and etiquette. An earlier use, that of Wykeham, designated that sphere of ethical obligation that cannot be compelled by law. Its proficients would show the moral knowledge and will, along with the social elegance (the moral and social were linked), of a true gentleperson, qualities implanted but also taught. Both senses of manners have long been thought distinctive of Edward Panosian. Another quality, humility, will certainly appear in his discomfort with my making these signature features, engrained and nurtured by God, he would rightly insist, so eagerly known.

> *Ron Horton has been on the faculty of Bob Jones University for fifty-nine years. He has authored books and specialized articles in his scholarly field as well as textbooks and other works for Christian education and for a Christian audience.*

PASTORS' TRIBUTES
by Dr. Alan Cairns

I don't think I will ever forget the night Dr. Panosian made his first appearance as Martin Luther. With a few well-chosen words, he immediately transported our church audience back into the sixteenth century and set about introducing us to the great German Reformer in the context of his own times. We felt as if Luther himself had paid us a visit, and by the time he came to the end of his story, the atmosphere in the service was like that of an evangelistic rally. What we had seen and heard was a work of sheer genius.

That is not too strong a word to use of Dr. Panosian, for it is no small achievement to present the world-changing events of church history in a way that captivates modern-day believers. Yet "genius" tells only a small part of the story. Others may speak with more immediate knowledge of his immense scholarship; I am content to speak of his godliness. I have known him for many years and have had the opportunity to see him up close and personal: a great man who is genuinely humble; a staunch, yet courteous defender of the faith;

a lover of the preached Word; a man of prayer; a gracious encourager of others, even when they wander into his field of expertise (as at times I did), when other professional historians may justifiably have found fault; like Barnabas, "a good man" whose many talents are entirely dedicated to the service of his Master.

I am delighted to know that the wider public will now have opportunity to learn more of Dr. Panosian's life and work. I have no doubt that as they gain an insight into his character they will not only admire him, but will learn more of the Christ to Whose service he has dedicated his life.

Alan Cairns is the Minister Emeritus of Faith Free Presbyterian Church in Greenville, South Carolina, where he served for almost thirty years. He is a respected preacher, an insightful author, and for many years the executive director of "Let the Bible Speak," the international radio ministry of the Free Presbyterian Church. He and Ed Panosian have been friends for over three decades.

---

by Pastor Greg Barkman

My first introduction to Dr. Ed Panosian was in Bob Jones Academy in the 1960's. I knew him as a performer with a remarkable deep voice. He seemed bigger than life, and I was awed by his commanding stage presence.

Entering the university in 1966 landed me in History of Civilization, a required course, where I experienced him as professor. I was mesmerized as he lectured for hours with no discernible notes. He possessed vast knowledge and an astounding memory. What a privilege to have been one of his students.

Years later, I invited him to our church in North Carolina to deliver a first-person biographical sketch of the life of Martin Luther. It was a thrill to introduce someone to our congregation who made a profound impression on me as a student. Over the years, he continued coming until he finally exhausted his repertoire of biographies. We eagerly anticipated each presentation, and gradually, our people developed an appreciation for church history by hearing him tell of Calvin, Hus, Zwingli, Knox, Whitefield, Spurgeon, and a host of others. It is impossible to overstate the interest he awakened in our people for the history of the church through the ages. He became a partner in ministry, and I am deeply grateful for his assistance.

Best of all, over the years, Ed and Betty Panosian became personal friends. Marti and I learned that he is everything in private that he appears to be in public, and more. By the working of God's grace, Ed Panosian is a genuinely godly and gracious man with a heart for Christ, truth, and others. I am blessed to have known this humble giant among men.

After completing training at Bob Jones University in 1972, Greg Barkman answered a call in 1973 to help a small group of believers begin a new Independent Baptist Church in Alamance County, North Carolina. Pastor Barkman has surpassed forty-five years of active pastoral ministry. He and his wife, Marti, have four married daughters, and nine grandchildren.

ACKNOWLEDGEMENTS

"In the multitude of counselors there is safety."

—Proverbs 11:14

This project has been immense, and it would have been impossible without the help of many. I owe them a great debt of gratitude.

First, Dr. Panosian has trusted me with his story and his good name. He has helped me by answering innumerable questions and emails. Mrs. Panosian has helped us remember facts from the stories of her husband's parents and shared details of her own life, despite her preference for privacy. And their daughter Lisa Panosian has been a tremendous aid in my endeavor to rightly comprehend and convey her parents' story. As both her father and she herself warned me, she is his greatest fan and therefore would be my greatest critic. She has kindly protected her parents, which I understand and admire, and which I believe helped improve the final product. I'm also indebted to Dr. Panosian's son Matthew and granddaughter Ghevont for collecting and scanning family pictures. To all the Panosians, "Thank you!"

Thank you to Hal Cook, who supervises Photo Services at BJU and helped me find many of the photographs included in the book. I'm grateful to Patrick Robbins, and especially to Jennifer Walton, who helped me navigate the archives of the BJU Library. Jennifer, you were eager to help however you could, even before or after hours. And thank you to Anna Fraley, who served as an eager researcher for me near the project's conclusion.

One of the most useful finds in the BJU Archives was a set of interviews Dr. John Matzko recorded with Dr. and Mrs. Panosian in July of 2002. They contain essentially the same stories I heard during my time with the Panosians, but often with some extra details. I've strewn quotations from those interviews throughout the book to supplement my own interaction with the Panosians. Thank you, Dr. Matzko!

Similarly, the transcript of a speech which Linda Hayner delivered at Dr. Panosian's retirement banquet on February 6, 2004, provided some very enjoyable anecdotes. Thank you!

Thank you to several friends who read the manuscript and offered suggestions for improvement. Those friends include Jamie Langston Turner, John Matzko, Rachel Larson, Tom Martin, Greg and Meredith Buckland, and others. Thank you all for investing your energy and insights into this project.

Many thanks to my mother, Jo Ellen Anderson, for tirelessly reviewing the first draft of the book and catching a scandalous number of typos and errors that had slipped my notice. My love for words and writing is genetic. Thank you, Mom!

Thank you to Ray Holden, soon to be my son-in-law. Ray served as a faithful courier on several occasions—copying manuscripts, taking a scrapbook and a computer back and forth between Atlanta and Greenville, and doing anything he could to move this project forward. I love you, Ray. Thanks for your servant's heart and continuous encouragement.

Thank you to three others who polished the manuscript until it shined. Abby Huffstutler is a trusted friend and my editor of choice. Thank you for your work on yet another of my projects. Joe Tyrpak was my assistant and my pastor when we served together at Tri-County Bible Church. Joe, I treasure your friendship, and I realize that your graphic design artistry has propelled Church Works Media forward for the last decade. Thank you for your labors as the artistic editor of the project, and especially for your excellent work on the book's cover. Finally, thank you to Jared Miller for working under Joe's leadership to complete the actual layout of the book's contents.

To my family—thank you for your forbearance during my six-month obsession with this project. You gave me space to write, read, and think. You shared my enthusiasm and listened to me drone on and on about life in Turkey over a hundred years ago. You tolerated my vacant looks at family meals when I was sorting through a detail of the story, and you understood when the meal abruptly ended as I rushed back to my study to capture an idea before it vanished. You rolled your eyes and shook your heads at me each evening when you said good-night, but you still understood my recklessly late nights, knowing I couldn't help but pursue this until it was finished. Now that this project has been completed, I look forward to some slow meals and long evenings together. We'll start with, "Hi, I'm your husband and your dad. Remember me?" Thank you for your support and encouragement, as crazy as I may be. I thank God for you.

BIBLIOGRAPHY

Aaron, Jeffrey. "Services Saturday for Elmira businessman Manny Panosian." *Star-Gazette* (Elmira, NY), January 28, 2015.

Adamic, Louis. *Laughing in the Jungle: The Autobiography of an American Immigrant.* New York: Harper and Brothers, 1932.

Ali, Ayaan Hirsi. "The Plot Behind Saudi Arabia's Fight with Qatar." *New York Times,* December 4, 2017.

"Alumni Appreciation Award." *Faith for the Family* 12, no. 2 (February 1984): 16.

Anbinder, Tyler. *City of Dreams: The 400-Year Epic History of Immigrant New York.* Boston, MA: Houghton Mifflin Harcourt, 2016.

Balakian, Grigoris. *Armenian Golgotha.* Translated by Peter Balakian with Aris Sevag. New York: Vintage Books, 2009.

Balakian, Peter. Introduction to *Armenian Golgotha.* Translated by Peter Balakian with Aris Sevag. New York: Vintage Books, 2009.

Balakian, Peter. *The Burning Tigris: The Armenian Genocide and America's Response.* New York, NY: HarperCollins Publishers, 2003.

Barton, Clara. *The Red Cross in Peace and War.* Washington, D.C.: American Historical Press, 1906.

"'Battle of Bull Run' Aired," *Voice of the Alumni* 35, no. 2 (September 1961): 2.

"BJU Faculty Are Chosen." *Voice of the Alumni* 46, no. 1 (June 1972): 2.

Bob Jones University. *Vintage.* Greenville, SC: 1983. BJU Archives.

Buchan, John. *A History of the Great War.* Boston, MA: Houghton Mifflin Company, n.d.

Calvin, John. *Institutes of the Christian Religion.* Edited by John T. McNeill. Translated by Ford Lewis Battles. Philadelphia: The Westminster Press, 1960.

Caner, Ergun Mehmet, and Emir Fethi Caner. *Unveiling Islam: An Insider's Look at Muslim Life and Beliefs.* Grand Rapids, MI: Kregel Publications, 2002.

Cannato, Vincent J. *American Passage: The History of Ellis Island.* New York, NY: Harper Perennial, 2010.

Carson, D. A. "What Is the Gospel?" Sermon delivered at The Gospel Coalition Conference, Trinity Evangelical Divinity School, Deerfield, IL, May 2007.

Chorbadjian, Smpat. *Surviving the Forgotten Armenian Genocide: A Moving Personal Story.* Edited by Patrick Sookhdeo. McLean, VA: Isaac Publishing, 2015.

Curti, Merle. *American Philanthropy Abroad.* New Brunswick, NJ: Rutgers University Press, 1963.

"Doctorates Conferred on BJU Faculty Pair." *Greenville Piedmont* (Greenville, SC), September 1, 1959.

Faculty Notes 2, no. 5 (February 1960): 2.

Fant, Clyde E., and Mitchell G. Reddish. *A Guide to Biblical Sites in Greece and Turkey.* New York: Oxford University Press, 2003.

Fornek, Kimberly. "Shoe Repair Shops Branch Out to Stay in Business." *Chicago Tribune,* December 19, 2016.

Freely, John. *Istanbul: The Imperial City.* London: Penguin Books, 1996.

Gilbert, Martin. *The First World War: A Complete History.* New York, NY: Henry Holt Company, 1994.

Green, Lucille B. "Actors Make 'Macbeth' Alive Again at BJU." *Greenville News* (Greenville, SC), May 27, 1967.

Green, Lucille B. "'Antigone' Skillfully Performed at BJU." *Greenville News* (Greenville, SC), 1965.

Green, Lucille B. "'Taming of Shrew' Called Lusty Comedy." *Greenville News* (Greenville, SC), May 28, 1971.

Greene, Frederick Davis. *The Armenian Crisis in Turkey: The Massacre of 1894, Its Antecedents and Significance.* New York: Knickerbocker Press, 1895.

Halsey, Francis Whiting. *The Literary Digest History of the World War.* Vol. VIII. New York: Funk & Wagnalls Company, 1919.

Harris, J. Rendel, and Helen B. Harris. *Letters from the Scenes of the Recent Massacres in Armenia.* New York: Fleming H. Revell, 1897.

Harris, William. *Lebanon: A History, 600–2001.* Oxford, England: Oxford University Press, 2012.

Hartley, Tom. "Armenian Refugee Found Success in America." *Star-Gazette* (Elmira, NY), May 6, 1969.

Hayner, Linda. Speech delivered at Dr. Panosian's Retirement Banquet, February 6, 2004.

Hines, Elena. "Faculty Love Stories Stir Hearts." *The Collegian* 12, no. 8 (February 4, 1999): 4.

Hosaflook, David. Editor's preface to *The Siege of Shkodra: Albania's Courageous Stand Against Ottoman Conquest, 1478.* Translated and edited by David Hosaflook. Tirana, Albania: Onufri Publishing House, 2012.

Jenkins, Philip. *The Great and Holy War: How World War I Became a Religious Crusade.* New York: Harper One, 2014.

Kasir, Sammir. *Beirut.* Translated by M. B. DeBevoise. Berkley, CA: University of California Press, 2010.

Keegan, John. *The First World War.* New York: Alfred A. Knopf, 1999.

Lloyd, Seton. *Ancient Turkey: A Traveler's History.* Berkley, CA: University of California Press, 1989.

MacKeen, Dawn Anahid. *The Hundred-Year Walk: An Armenian Odyssey*. New York: Houghton Mifflin Harcourt, 2016.

Meyer, G. J. *A World Undone: The Story of the Great War 1914 to 1918*. New York: Bantam Books, 2015.

Montgomery, Lucy Maud. *The Story Girl*. Boston: L. C. Page, 1911.

Morgenthau, Henry. *Ambassador Morgenthau's Story*. Self-published, CreateSpace, 2017.

Mowat, Barbara, Paul Werstine, Michael Poston, and Rebecca Niles, eds. *Hamlet*. Washington: Folger Shakespeare Library, n.d. Accessed August 27, 2018. www.folgerdigitaltexts.org.

Mowat, Barbara, Paul Werstine, Michael Poston, and Rebecca Niles, eds. *The Taming of the Shrew*. Washington: Folger Shakespeare Library, n.d. Accessed August 27, 2018. www.folgerdigitaltexts.org.

"Nazar Panosian Dies." *Star-Gazette* (Elmira, NY): n.d.

"Outstanding Educators of America." *Voice of the Alumni* 44, no. 4. (December 1970): 7.

Panosian, Betty. Interview by John Matzko, July 5 and 11, 2002. BJU Archives.

Panosian, Edward M. "A Case for History in the Christian School." *The Providence of God in History*. Greenville, SC: BJU Press, 1996.

Panosian, Edward. Interview by John Matzko, July 15 and 17, 2002. BJU Archives.

Panosian, Edward M. *Islam and the Bible: Considering Islam Biblically*. Greenville, SC: Emerald House Group, 2003.

"Panosians to Celebrate 50th Wedding Anniversary." *Star-Gazette* (Elmira, NY): n.d.

Ramsay, William. *Impressions of Turkey During Twelve Years' Wanderings*. London: Hodder & Stoughton-Aberdeen University Press, 1897.

Rowland, Gil. "What's Doing: BJU Drama Has Audience Breathless; May Provoke Argument." *Greenville Piedmont* (Greenville, SC), November 29, 1968.

Royde-Smith, John Graham. "World War I: Killed, Wounded, and Missing." *Encyclopedia Britannica.* www.britannica.com/event/World-War-I/Killed-wounded-and-missing. Accessed August 27, 2018.

Ryle, J. C. *Thoughts for Young Men.* Edinburgh, UK: The Banner of Truth Trust, 2016.

Sookhdeo, Patrick. Foreword and conclusion to *Surviving the Forgotten Armenian Genocide: A Moving Personal Story.* McLean, VA: Isaac Publishing, 2015.

Spenser, Edmund. *The Faerie Queene,* V.ii.39.9. https://scholarsbank. uoregon.edu/xmlui/bitstream/handle/1794/784/faeriequeene.pdf. Accessed August 27, 2018.

Turner, Daniel L. *Standing without Apology: The History of Bob Jones University.* Greenville, SC: BJU Press, 2001.

U.S. Immigration Act of 1907. Available at https://www.loc.gov/law/help/statutes-at-large/59th-congress/session-2/c59s2ch1134.pdf. Accessed August 8, 2018.

Werfel, Franz. *The Forty Days of Musa Dagh.* Translated by Geoffrey Dunlop and James Reidel. Boston, MA: Verba Mundi Books, 2012.

"Yearbooks Dedicated." *Faith for the Family* 11, no. 6 (July/August 1983): 18.

Yost, Gail. "The Experience of a Lifetime." *The Voice of the Alumni* 76, no. 5 (Spring 2003): 14.

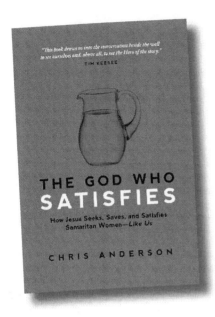

"In this little book, a gifted poet transitions to prose. I have known Chris Anderson for over two decades, first as a student and then as a fellow laborer in the work of the Kingdom. This book's focus on the Samaritan woman is full of Christ and the glorious gospel of grace. Written in an easy-to-read, popular style full of real-life illustrations, the book effectively links helpful background facts and precisely-stated theological truths to experiential application. It is a book that can be used for evangelism as well as for warming the believer's heart to renewed gratitude for what Christ has abundantly supplied."

—**Michael P. V. Barrett**, dean and professor at Puritan Reformed Theological Seminary and author of *Complete in Him* and *Beginning at Moses*

"This DVD documentary represents an excellent introduction to the life and ministry of the famed missionary. Together the interviewees paint a picture of Brainerd that is informed by the best scholarship, is honest about his various struggles and failures, but remains warmly sympathetic to Brainerd's life, thought, and missionary zeal. The film itself reflects quality craftsmanship and includes many beautiful shots of locations that were prominent in Brainerd's life, original manuscripts of his writings, and portraits, statues, and other memorials of figures discussed in the documentary. The film should prove a helpful resource for use in local church Sunday School classes, small groups, and discussion groups."

—**Nathan A. Finn**, dean and professor at Union University and writer for the Jonathan Edwards Center at Trinity Evangelical Divinity School

Gospel Meditations for Women

"Wrestling with guilt and frustration, far too many Christian women are living below the privileges of their spiritual inheritance. The solution is not found in any strengthened resolve of duty, but rather in having souls settled in the blessed liberty of Christ through the sweet enjoyment of the gospel. A union of sound doctrine and practical teaching, *Gospel Meditations for Women* beautifully highlights those unbinding messages of grace that so powerfully ignite joyful passion for Christ and holy living. What an invaluable resource!"

—**Holly Stratton**, conference speaker and blogger at *LifeHurts.us*

Gospel Meditations for Men

"A full month of meaty, masculine meditations. This is a wonderful resource for men seeking to deepen their understanding and build spiritual stamina. Each day's reading is a rich feast. Devotional material of this quality for men is extremely hard to come by!"

—**Phil Johnson**, executive director of Grace to You, and the founder of *Pyromaniacs* and *www.spurgeon.org*

Gospel Meditations for Missions

"By almost any standard—the intentionality of local churches to train, assess, and prepare prospective missionaries; the length of time it takes a missionary to raise support; the little sense of gospel partnership we have with the missionaries we do support—Western Christians don't do missions very well. The reason we don't do missions well is that we've not thought about missions well. This book has our poor thinking about missions in its crosshairs."

—**Matthew Hoskinson**, pastor of The First Baptist Church in New York City and author of *Assurance of Salvation*

Gospel Meditations for Prayer

"Brief and biblical, these meditations are full of sharp edges. They lead us to pray as cross-bearing disciples of Christ. Yet Anderson, Tyrpak, and Trueman comfort us with Christ's perfect grace for fallen people. So *Gospel Meditations for Prayer* is an encouraging book, but one designed to stretch you."

—**Joel Beeke**, president of Puritan Reformed Theological Seminary, Grand Rapids, and editor of *Taking Hold of God: Reformed and Puritan Perspectives on Prayer*

Gospel Meditations for the Hurting

"These meditations are Word-centered prescriptions that blow away the meaningless Christian platitudes often used to mask unanswerable pain. Until that day when Christ Himself wipes away all tears from our eyes, the Scriptures provide strength, help, and hope in this broken world. Let this book guide you to Christ, the only sure and lasting Refuge."

—**Tim Keesee**, author of the *Dispatches from the Front* DVD series and book and executive director of Frontline Missions International

Gospel Meditations for Christmas

"This work is more than a mere devotional and collection of meditations for Christmas. These meditations are a mini Christology. I hope they will be read far beyond December. There is too much truth here to be relegated to the Christmas season alone. I highly recommend this work for your greater understanding and worship of Jesus Christ."

—**Rick Holland**, pastor of Mission Road Bible Church, Kansas City, and professor of Homiletics at The Expositor's Seminary

35754394R00122

Made in the USA
Columbia, SC
26 November 2018